*Elisabeth and Her Cousin, Mary
Tell the Stories of Their Sons' Births*

Betty B. Howard

God's Gift of Love

Elisabeth and Mary, Mothers of
John the Baptist and Jesus
Tell the Stories of Their Sons' Births
By Betty B. Howard

First Edition
Copyright © 2001 by Betty B. Howard

Bible quotations from the KJV of <u>The Bible</u>. with antiquated terms updated by Betty B. Howard.

No part of the book (except Bible verses from the KJV in Appendix D) may be reproduced or transmitted in any form or any means, electronic or mechanical, including photocopying, recording or by any information storage and retrieval system, without written permission from the author, except for the inclusion of brief quotations in a review.

Published by
The Good News Connection, Inc.
2875 S. Orange Avenue, Suite 500-2500
Orlando, FL 32806-5455 U.S.A.
www.TheGoodNewsConnection.com

ISBN 0-9714057-6-X

Printed in the United States of America

Dedication

This book is dedicated to God,
The Father, for His great love,
The Son, for His great sacrifice, and
The Holy Spirit, for His great revelation.

To my dear husband, Bob, for all his love, prayers,
assistance and encouragement,
To the rest of our family: our youngest daughter, Marcia,
who has been close with so much help and joy,
Our oldest daughter, Valerie, her husband, Paul,
their six children,
Our middle daughter, Julie, her husband, Ben,
and their five children
All are far more precious to me than mere words can express.

And this dedication would be incomplete
without a dedication
To all my supportive brothers and sisters
in the family of God,
who have made this book possible

Acknowledgments

My sincere thanks are due to the many people who have prayed for, encouraged and helped me to produce this book, made connections for me and otherwise assisted me in various ways:

> To my husband, Bob, who has read numerous prepublication revisions for grammatical accuracy,
> To Morris and Ann Barwick, my brother and sister-in-law, for all their help in making this book possible.
> To Dr. Bill Jones, for wading through the first rough draft and his suggestions
> To Dr. Grady McMurtry for his advice on Jewish customs and law, and
> To K.O. and Susan Taylor for their suggestions and many prayers,

My regrets that I can not list all the many brothers and sisters in the Lord who have come along side me in writing this book but the Lord knows their names and I pray His richest blessings on them.

Contents

Preface ix
Introduction xi
1 Memories of Better Times 1
   Elisabeth Remembers the Happiness in Her Early Years of Marriage
2 Lord, Hear my Prayer 7
   Elisabeth Grieves Over Her Childlessness
3 Serving the Lord 10
   The Priesthood of Zacharias
4 A Heavenly Visitor 18
   The Lord Breaks His 400 Years of Silence
5 A Visitor with a Heavenly Message 24
   Elisabeth Has an Unexpected Visit from Mary
6 Lord, Help Us Understand How We Fit into Your Plan 29
   Mary Stays with Elisabeth for Three Months
7 *He Shall be Called John* 33
   Zacharias' and Elisabeth's Baby is Born
8 But What About Mary 37
   She was Found to be With Child
9 *In the Fulness of Time* 43
   Mary Gives Birth
10 Shepherds Seek the Lamb 50
   Angels Announce the Baby's Birth to Shepherds
11 Circumcision of the Baby 55
   His name was called JESUS
12 Presentation in the Temple 58
   Simeon and Anna Bless the Baby
13 *A Star in the East* 61
   A Visit from the Wise Men
14 Home at Last 67
   He Shall be Called a Nazarene

Appendices

Appendix A   Biblical Marriage Customs: A Picture of the Relationship Of the Bride of Christ to her Groom 77

Appendix B   Anna the Prophetess, an Intercessor for Baby Jesus: How to Pray and to Develop a Prayer Notebook for Children 86

Appendix C   Study Suggestions for Scriptures on the Births of John The Baptist and Jesus 93

Appendix D   Scriptures from Matthew and Luke on the Births of John the Baptist and Jesus without Commentary 98

Bibliography   112

Preface

*For God so loved the world that
he gave his only begotten son...*
John 3:16

Jesus, God's Gift of Love

Just two lines but so full of meaning. Men and women have spent lifetimes trying to comprehend this great love of the Father, all the while sensing the inability fully to understand it in this life. God, so loving and so attentive to detail, planned the giving of His Son before the foundation of the world. With the beginning of time, all history was aimed toward His Son's coming in human form and His ultimate sacrifice.

He created the Jewish nation, a select people, through which His Son would come. He arranged people and all historical events so that Jesus would come in the fullness of time. This book is about the two women He prepared for the first advent. It was not an accident that Elisabeth was past childbearing years before she bore her son, John, who would prepare the way for the Lord. It was part of the Lord's design to show that when humans reach the end of their resources, He not only moves but does so in such a mighty way that it is beyond what mere man can do.

This story begins with Elisabeth and the grief she experienced during her childless years. She steps to the stage to share with those in the twenty-first century her struggles and then her joy in answered prayer. Next, Mary, the mother of Jesus takes center stage and the spotlight to tell her story of Jesus' birth. Her joy, wonder and complete submission as a handmaid of the Lord are inspirations for all time.

Enter now into the first century and learn of the people God chose for His powerful detailed work and His Gift of Love for the world in giving His only begotten Son.

Introduction

Several years ago, while I was researching the scriptures for a Bible study on the births of John the Baptist and Jesus, I was drawn to Elisabeth. I could not forget these two lines:

> *And they had no child, because Elisabeth*
> *was barren,*
> *And they were both well stricken in years.*
> Luke 1:7

The more I meditated on this verse, the more I began to sense the heartache of this couple during the years they were childless. The usual cursory reading of these lines does not always reveal the decades of heartache and loss they must have endured before the announcement that Elisabeth would have a son. The more I thought of their circumstances, the more the story came alive to me. After research and meditation on their plight that eventually turned to joy, I decided to write about insights that came to me. While this book was originally drafted to tell the story of Elisabeth, it was obviously incomplete without the story of Mary, her cousin. And so developed the story of the births of John the Baptist and Jesus as told by their mothers, Elisabeth and her cousin, Mary.

While interest in this topic may be higher around the Christmas season, it really is a story for all seasons. Hopefully there are new insights here into a narrative most believers have heard many times over. Almost all Bible verses from Matthew and Luke, which relate to the births of John the Baptist and Jesus, have been included and written in italics. Scriptural references are from the King James Version. This author updated antiquated words; such as thee, thou, ye, etc. The term, "Holy Ghost" has been changed to "Holy Spirit."

Sometimes in this story, a New Testament verse will be attributed to one of the characters who lived before its writing. The principles of the Word are timeless and existed even before the writing of the New Testament so words given to these characters were not done without careful thought.

There are several ways this book may be used:

Some may want to read just the text of the story to glean enjoyment and inspiration then stop there.

Others may want to read further into the appendix, using various sections, which may be of interest to them.

Appendix A springs from <u>marriage customs</u> shown in the main text in the lives of Elisabeth and Zacharias, then Mary and Joseph. Building on this are other illustrations shown in the Bible that illustrate the glorious picture of the relationship of the Bride of Christ to her Groom. Hopefully, this will be an inspiration to all Christians awaiting that great heavenly wedding feast with their Groom.

Appendix B contains directions for developing <u>a prayer notebook for children</u> and comes from the character Anna, the prophetess, introduced in the main text as an intercessor for Baby Jesus. Here readers will find directions for becoming intercessors for children they know by developing a prayer notebook consisting of Bible verses turned into prayers. This will give a written testimony as a heritage for those children to know what has been prayed for them.

Appendix C contains <u>study suggestions</u> for anyone wanting to study further the Scriptures on the births of John the Baptist and Jesus. Students doing personal study, classroom teachers, home Bible study leaders or homeschooling parents can use the main text of this book as an interest builder for these verses. However, these people may instead want to do an inductive study (one which begins with the Word of God before going to other resources) and start their study with the verses found in Appendix D. In that appendix are Scriptures of these births written in the generally accepted chronological order. After a thorough study of these verses, the main text of this book can then be read as a commentary, along with other resources that give commentary on the same Scriptures.

Appendix D contains the <u>Bible verses from Matthew and Luke</u> used in this book. They are included in chronological order without commentary except for titles of each section. It is important for the reader to reread these scriptures, without written commentary, in order to have a clear understanding of what is the Word of God and what has been presented in this book as the author's comments.

My prayer is that all who read this will come away with new insights and revelation into Jesus Christ, the Father's Gift of Love, and respond with a greater love for Him.

Betty B. Howard
Ephesians 3:20, 21
September, 2001

Chapter 1
Memories of Better Times

Elisabeth Remembers the Happiness in Her Early Years of Marriage

And they had no child, because that Elisabeth was barren, and they both were now well stricken in years.
Luke 1:7

Elisabeth slowly lifted the water jar to her slightly stooped shoulder as she prepared for her daily trip to the well. Her work worn hand brushed a strand of gray hair from her lined forehead. Oh, how she dreaded these trips! She dreaded seeing the mothers with their children laughing and playing together. Her arms ached and her heart was empty because for some reason the Lord had closed her womb and after decades of marriage she still had no child. She dreaded the faces full of pity as they watched her with her chore. The pain was almost unbearable when she heard the whispers, "Isn't it too bad that Elisabeth is barren?" With her jar full of water she would hurry home as fast as one of her advanced age could with such a heavy load, but by the time she arrived home, the water coursing down her cheeks was not spilling from the jar but from her tears.

How different these daily trips were over forty-five years ago when she and her husband, Zacharias, were first married! At that

> *There was in the days of Herod, the king of Judea, a certain priest named Zacharias, of the course of Abia: and his wife was of the daughters of Aaron, and her name was Elisabeth.*
> — Luke 1:5

time she eagerly looked forward to the trips...to visit with the other women and to catch up on the latest news. The children would run to meet her, eager to have a hug from her. Young mothers were even more eager to share about the baby who got his first tooth or one who took his first step. She rejoiced whenever a shy wife announced that she just found out she was with child. "Oh," she thought, "One day I will be the one to make that announcement and I will birth a child for Zacharias." Then Elisabeth would let her imagination soar as she would see in her mind's eye all the children; especially boys, she would be bringing to the well each day. But at that time in her early marriage, her joy was complete in being the wife to a husband who would one day be a priest and in making a home for him. Because Zacharias was of the tribe of Levi and since Elisabeth's family were descendents of Aaron, the union was a special blessing for Zacharias, too.[1]

Elisabeth's engagement and wedding followed the customs of her day. While some brides in her day were in their early teens, Elisabeth was in her middle teens and Zacharias around twenty at the time of their engagement. After their parents were assured their children were in agreement with the union-to-be, Zacharias' father arranged their betrothal with her father. The betrothal was finalized with the giving of money and gifts along with an exchange of oaths, celebrated with a feast in Elisabeth's home and followed by a year of engagement. Even though the engagement was as binding as marriage and he was known as her husband and she, his wife, they did not live together nor have any physical relations during that time.[2] In fact, for that period, communication between Elisabeth and Zacharias was never face to face but only through a friend of the bridegroom.[3] After the betrothal festivities,

Zacharias' parting words to Elisabeth were, "I am going to prepare a place for you, and when all things are ready, I will come again, and receive you unto myself."[4] Those words were indelibly engraved on her heart and almost daily she mentally rehearsed them, yearning for the time he would come.

It was a year of preparation and anticipation for both. Zacharias was working to make ready the modest home, adjacent to his father's house[5] in which he would one day take his bride, and Elisabeth did all that was necessary to make herself ready to be his bride. After the wedding ceremony they would then enjoy rights God has reserved for only a husband and wife at that time. Her hope was not only for that day he would take his bride home but expectation of the time she would bear his children and possibly be the mother of that special One for Whom all Israel was looking.

Elisabeth's childhood had adequately prepared her to be the wife of a priest. Because Elisabeth was a descendent of Aaron, and the men in her family were of the priesthood, they regularly gathered in her childhood home with discussions that thrilled her. Often they spoke of the Lord, His Word, stories of the Patriarchs, Moses, the exploits of Joshua, the glory of Israel under King David, the singing of his psalms, the beauty of King Solomon's Temple, and the prophecies of the Messiah, the Hope of Israel. Admittedly, the completion of her childhood household duties was sometimes delayed as she lingered to overhear these men speak of such great things.

One of the prophesies of which the men often spoke was from the prophet Isaiah, *"Therefore the Lord himself will give you a sign; Behold, a virgin shall conceive, and bear a son, and shall call his name Immanuel."*[6] It was obvious no one had an understanding of how this could be. Another question the men often discussed was, "When and how will the Lord restore Israel?" She, too, wondered with these men, as well as the rest of Israel. Yes, they were living in the Promised Land, but it had been centuries since the glorious rule of King David and his son, King Solomon. The rule of the Romans would surely someday be overthrown, probably by the Promised Messiah, and the kingdom restored.

What a blessing to be the woman God would choose as the Messiah's mother! Was she, as a child, being irreverent or even blasphemous longing to be that woman when she grew up? During the engagement year the thought occasionally found its way into her mind that hopefully, she would be the mother to bear Immanuel. This was something so special in her thinking, so private, that she dare not share it with anyone lest she be the subject of ridicule. She also chided herself for thinking she might be the blessed one who would bear the Messiah! She must keep in mind that the Lord's ways are not our ways.

The yearlong engagement finally ended and the anticipated week of wedding celebration with friends and family arrived. The friend of the bridegroom had kept Elisabeth informed during the year as to Zacharias' progress on their home. Now that their dwelling place was finished, the friend alerted her that Zacharias would be coming one evening but did not indicate the hour. On that appointed evening she was aglow with the radiance which seems reserved only for brides. She nervously "arrayed" herself "in fine linen, clean and white"[7] a dress "with no spot or wrinkle"[8] for this longed for occasion. Her virgin friends, carrying their lamps filled with oil, gathered in her home at sundown to await his arrival.[9]

When Zacharias set out that evening for Elisabeth's house to take her to his, "he was dressed in a festive dress with a handsome turban on his head and a nuptial crown."[10] He had a band of merry makers with him. He was attended by his groomsman, and companions and they all were followed by a band of musicians and singers. When they finally reached the home of Elisabeth at midnight, she was surrounded by her maidens, and all were anxiously expecting his arrival.[11] The cry came, "Behold, the bridegroom comes" and the maidens "arose and trimmed their lamps" because it was late and "went out to meet him."[12]

With Elisabeth veiled and by his side, and lamps lighting the way, Zacharias conducted the whole joyous party from her home back to his. On the way they were joined by a party of "maidens, friends of the bride and bridegroom, who were in waiting to watch the procession as it passed."[13] It was a happy time when family, friends and neighbors, all wearing wedding garments, arrived at Zacharias' house for the gala. In due time, "the bride was conducted to the bridal chamber"[14] and the marriage consummated. Then a week of feasting, blessings and gifts followed, enlivened with riddles and other amusements. Now that Zacharias had entered into direct communication with Elisabeth, his friend, who had been the intermediary during the engagement, regarded as a satisfactory testimony the success of his share of the work when he heard the voice of the bridegroom conversing with her.[15]

So began the marriage of this fine young couple. Elizabeth obviously did not conceive the Holy One. Her hopes that she might have been His mother were so private she didn't even share them with her dear husband. But there were enough blessings just in being Zacharias' wife and building a home with him that for now, nothing else mattered.

They lived in a city in the hill country of Juda just a few miles from Jerusalem. Later, when Zacharias would be required to perform his priestly duties in Jerusalem, which he would begin when he was thirty, it would be convenient to travel there. Elisabeth liked having a home next to her husband's family. Zacharias was the kind of husband most women would desire, because he would be a priest and they would be provided for adequately; also, he was wise, kind, gentle and strong. Most

> *And they were both righteous before God, walking in all the commandments and ordinances of the Lord blameless.*
> ⸺ Luke 1:6

of all, he loved God just as she did and she rejoiced that once again she lived in a home where the Lord and His Word were such an integral part of daily life. She could not even imagine anything else. As Zacharias shared the Scriptures with her every day it was as though she were *washed daily with the water of the Word.*[16] Even from early marriage their desire was always to be *righteous before God, walking in all the commandments and ordinances of the Lord blameless.*[17]

Zacharias was one of the learned young men in the tribe of Levi and he was well versed in the stories of the Patriarchs, in the promises of God to them, in the Law of Moses and the prophets. Elisabeth never tired of listening to the stories she had heard as a child: of Abraham, Isaac, Jacob, Joseph, Samuel, King David, Isaiah and their faith in God. The story of Abraham always intrigued her. What faith he had! After waiting so long for the promised son, he could willingly give up his son because of that faith. He believed God would bring his son back from the dead.[18] Only someone of great faith could have thought of such a new concept, much less believed in it, because no one had ever come back to life at that time!

What did Sarah (mother of Isaac) think when her beloved son was to be sacrificed by his father, like the pagans around them offered their children to pagan gods? Did Abraham even tell her where he and Isaac were going when they left for a three day journey to Mount Moriah?[19] If so, did she have the faith to believe Isaac would come back? The Scriptures did not say that Sarah knew. These are things that only a woman would consider, but Elisabeth loved to meditate on such things, even though she may never know the answer.

Their first year of marriage flew by so quickly both husband and wife could hardly believe it. The only thing they found surprising was that by their first anniversary Elisabeth was not with child. Other young wives in their city had conceived and delivered during that time and she was sure she would be next in expecting a child. She encouraged and reassured herself there was plenty of time and surely in this next year she would bear a child. But, alas, that year passed and no baby came to bless their home.

Chapter 2

Lord, Hear my Prayer

Elisabeth Grieves Over Her Childlessness

Hear me when I call, O God of my righteousness...Have mercy upon me, and hear my prayer.
Psalm 4:1

Elisabeth had plenty to do with all her own household chores: cleaning, marketing, preparing food in accordance with the Law of Moses, making daily trips to the well to draw water, making clothes for her husband, herself and so on. But she also helped any of her neighbors who were sick and assisted mothers in taking care of their little ones; like baby Samuel, three months old, who lived next door with his mother, Rebekah, and his father, Reuben. Just a few houses from Elisabeth lived a childhood friend of hers (also named Elisabeth but called Beth) who gave birth to three daughters in four years. That mother certainly needed help! But at the end of the day, Elisabeth had to return to her childless home with expectations that it was only a matter of time before she would birth her own child to hold in her arms.

But the passing months soon turned into years of childlessness, which caused Zacharias and Elisabeth to become more than just a little anxious. Many nights she cried herself to sleep.

Zacharias often held her in his arms while reassuring her that surely he would fill any void in her life. Even as Elkanah, Hannah's husband tried to comfort Hannah, so Zacharias tried to comfort Elisabeth.[1] While he had a big part of her heart, still there was that spot placed in a woman's heart by God only a child could fill. As more and more years passed with no baby she often wondered if she or Zacharias had committed some sin, which caused the Lord to close her womb and withhold the blessing of children.

Often she found herself thinking of Hannah, Samuel's mother, who had been barren because the Lord had also closed her womb. Elisabeth experienced teasing for her reproach from thoughtless friends and relatives. At those times she was reduced to tears. Of course, her thoughtless teasers did not say a word in front of Zacharias because he was very protective of her. During those difficult times, when there was no one to comfort or protect her, she would remember how Hannah had been verbally tormented to tears over her barrenness.[2] Elisabeth concluded that surely since Hannah had prayed and the Lord had not only opened her womb but also sent her such a special son as Samuel, plus many more children, He would do the same for her.[3] So she prayed even more ... but still no baby.

While this burden of a childless home may appear as though it was only Elisabeth's, it was extremely difficult for Zacharias, too. He, also, had to rejoice with other husbands as they announced with great joy, their wives were expecting babies. He, too, had to be around friends and family members sharing the joys of milestones in the lives of their children. As the sons of his fellow priests grew up in preparation for the priesthood, his heart, likewise, was broken for a son or sons he never had, whom he could have loved and trained to be priests. It would have been a joy to teach his children the words of the Lord diligently *when* he *sat in* his *house, and when* he *walked by the way, and when* he *lay down and when* he *rose up.* He would have taught them to *love the Lord thy God with all your heart, and with all your soul, and with all your might,* because *these words which* the Lord *had commanded ... were in* Zacharias' *heart.* These words were not only written on his heart but like all Jews were also *written on the posts of his house and on his gates.* [4]

Yes, Zacharias, himself yearned to have a family like others around him. He carried his own private burden but he knew he must be strong for his wife who might be in tears at any moment over her reproach. The law allowed him to divorce his wife over this childlessness but he loved Elisabeth too much to do that.[5] He would bear this burden with her while trusting God for this, just as they trusted Him with everything else in their lives.

When the couple first realized that not bearing children was becoming a problem, Zacharias remembered that Isaac and Rebekah had been married twenty years before having children. He recalled *Isaac prayed for his wife because she was barren; and the Lord answered his prayer and Rebekah, his wife conceived.*[6] Isaac's answered prayer was not just one child, but twins, Esau and Jacob! And so Zacharias prayed, drawing faith from the Word of God, that the Lord would open Elisabeth's womb, but still no child.

As the years passed, Elizabeth recalled Sarah's plight more and more. What Sarah (at that time named Sarai) must have gone through during those years she could not bear a child for her husband, Abraham, (named Abram during those years) to whom God had promised a descendent! Abraham, an example of faith, must have been Sarah's strength, too. He was strong in faith during those childless years, knowing that a faith that changes because circumstances change, is faith in the circumstances, not faith in God, Who never changes.[7] But the years were passing rapidly for Elisabeth and she was nearing the end of childbearing years, so hope for her was almost gone. After all, she and Zacharias had no special promise for a child like Abraham and Sarah had from an angelic visitor.[8]

Chapter 3

Serving the Lord

The Priesthood of Zacharias

There was in the days of Herod, king of Judea, a certain priest named Zacharias.
Luke 1:5

Zacharias was engrossed those years with his priestly duties. During that time Herod the Great rebuilt and expanded the Temple in Jerusalem. The original Temple built by King Solomon was glorious in all its splendor, not just because of its material beauty but because of the presence of the Lord. Over the centuries that followed its construction, the rich furnishings and decorations were gradually stripped away. Periodically efforts were made to restore it. There were times, to the shame of the Jewish nation, pagan worship was even practiced there.[1] The prophet Ezekiel had prophesied that a time would come when Israel's idolatrous worship would be so repugnant to the Holy One of Israel His Spirit would depart from the Temple. That time came and the Spirit left and had never returned. With the Spirit gone, the buildings were soon gone, too. When the Chaldeans destroyed Jerusalem, they pillaged its remaining valuables before burning it to the ground.

The Temple rebuilt by the children of Israel after their return from Babylonian Captivity also suffered over the centuries from pillage and defilement with idolatrous worship. Aside from the missing splendor of the Temple, again, the biggest loss was the presence of God and the Ark of the Covenant. Needless to say, the Holy of Holies was empty and only the Lord Himself knew where the Ark was or if it even existed. Although this Temple was restored, it was taken again by Pompey, and later by Herod the Great. The Temple Herod captured was one in great disrepair. Herod had concluded that it would be to his advantage to keep the large Jewish population happy so they would not cause trouble, plus he was a master builder with numerous buildings to his credit. "The Temple as it existed after the captivity was not such as would satisfy a man as vain and fond of display as Herod the Great; and he accordingly undertook the task of rebuilding it on a grander scale."[2]

Herod, a tyrannical ruler, was also one of the most evil men ever to live. His wicked heart was expressed in committing numerous atrocities. His insane lust for power had driven him to murder his favorite wife, to murder his own sons as well as his best friend and thousands of others for fear they would try to overthrow him. Is it any wonder the Jews hated him? After preparation for rebuilding, work on the Temple began in King Herod's 18th year of reign (20 or 21 B.C.).[3] It was the Lord's timing to restore the Temple and He could even use a man as wicked as Herod the Great. The Lord used this evil civil ruler in spite of his wickedness, as well as He uses others to accomplish His purposes.

Now that repairs were completed, once again the Jewish people could restore more fully Mosaic sacrifices and worship in the Temple. There was an air of expectation in all Israel because of this newly refurbished Temple but it seemed more than that. It seemed as though the Lord were preparing for something beyond what finite man's mind could fathom.

For over four hundred long silent years the Lord had not spoken directly to His people. Worse yet, the last time He spoke, He spoke through the prophet Malachi with these ominous words, *Behold, I will send you Elijah the prophet before the coming of the great and dreadful day of the* LORD. *And he shall turn the heart of the fathers to the children, and the heart of the children to their fathers, lest I come and smite the earth with a curse.*[4] Every time Elisabeth participated in preparations for the Passover Supper she remembered that prophecy when she placed the cup for Elijah on the table. Surely now, with the restoration of the Temple, the Lord would break His silence and send Elijah to turn the fathers and children to each other.

Zacharias belonged to one of the twenty-four divisions of priests that King David had organized. "There were as many as twenty thousand priests altogether and so there were not far short of a thousand in each section."[5]

While twenty of the divisions had been part of the lost tribes, which did not return after the captivity, there was a reorganization of those who did return so all twenty-four family names existed again.

...A certain priest named Zacharias, of the course of Abia...
Luke 1:5

Because there were so many priests this organization was necessary. Zacharias was not of the family Abia but belonged to the division which bore that name.[6]

He traveled to Jerusalem one week twice a year for priestly duties with his division; one week in the first half of the year and one week in the second half. He also journeyed there for three feasts; Passover, Pentecost and Tabernacles when attendance by all priests was required.[7] All Jewish men were required to attend these feasts, too, and sometimes the men would take their wives and children. Those times were great for worshipping the Lord, for reunion of friends and family members and to catch up with all the latest family and political news.

Those times Elisabeth journeyed to Jerusalem with Zacharias were bittersweet for her. She loved worshipping the Lord at the Temple and being with the distant relatives and friends but as always, she was painfully reminded she had no children while friends and relatives had many and sometimes a house full!

Everyone loved Elisabeth. People, old and young alike, were attracted to her sweet spirit. There was one young cousin, who especially loved her and her name was Mary. Mary's family lived in Nazareth. Elisabeth had been in Jerusalem when Mary's family made the lengthy pilgrimage and first brought her as a young child to that city. Year after year Elisabeth and Zacharias had watched Mary grow. Often Mary and her family had been in their home. Many times, after the family left, Zacharias and Elisabeth could not help but remark about Mary being such an unusual child. They could not exactly identify her unique qualities, but both agreed there was a purity, almost a holiness about her like no other child they had known. It was obvious that Mary, even at her tender age, loved the Lord. Surely, He would one day bless her with a devoted husband and a house full of children for it was apparent that she will make the perfect mother.

On those trips to Jerusalem, Elisabeth spent as much time as she could around the Temple; usually in the court of women just outside the Temple. Again she reflected on Abraham, who thousands of years earlier, was so willing to offer his son, Isaac, on this spot, Mount Moriah, which was in the wilderness at the time of the offering.[8] Oh, for a faith like that!

Elizabeth had never been inside the Holy Pace, because only priests were allowed there, so certainly no woman was permitted in. But Zacharias' very detailed description gave her a vision that was so vivid, she could almost believe she had seen it with her own eyes. He had carefully described to her everything inside the Holy Place; from the table of shewbread, to the golden lampstand and the altar of incense just in front of the thick curtain which separated the Holy Place from the Holy of Holies. Zacharias had never been inside the Holy of Holies, because that was reserved for the High Priests, who went in just once a year. And sadly since the ark of the covenant had never been found, the Holy of Holies was empty.

There was one woman Elisabeth sought out sometimes during her trips. The woman's name was Anna, who was called a prophetess, from the daughter of Phanuel and of the tribe of Asher. Her husband had died only seven years after their wedding and now, Anna, as a widow, spent all her time at the Temple in fastings and prayers, night and day.* Some people might have tagged her as eccentric but for Elisabeth, Anna was a woman who had chosen the good life. A radiance emitted from the woman, a radiance described by Elisabeth as that which only comes from being in the presence of God through continuing prayer.

While Elisabeth cherished being in the Temple area she did not like the moneychangers who exchanged money for travelers needing the Hebrew half shekel for the annual Temple tax.[9] This was supposed to be a service for Jews coming from long distances but it was obvious these men were very shady, greedy and just plain evil. She and Zacharias never did business with them. Everyone knew they took advantage of travelers. How it must grieve the Lord for these men to make wicked merchandise at this place of worship! She made it a point to quicken her pace when she passed the tables of the moneychangers and always breathed a sigh of relief when they were out of her sight.

There were some other people in the Temple area, who troubled her but these were people for whom she had compassion not disdain. First, at the Gate called Beautiful, there was a lad, lame from birth, who was carried and laid there daily to beg alms.** Elisabeth had to pass through this gate often for it was the principle entrance into the Court of Women.[10] She and Zacharias always gave him alms. Not only did she give him money she also silently offered a prayer for the Lord to meet his needs. A little farther away from the Temple area, on the side some distance from the Pool of Siloam, was a young blind man in his early teens, also afflicted from birth. Her heart went out to him, knowing he could never provide for himself, much less a family. His parents would lead him to the Gate where he sat daily, begging money.*** Again, Elisabeth would see that he received some from their family's income. She was not exactly sure how to pray for him, but she did pray the Lord would have mercy on him and somehow be glorified by his life.

* We meet her years later in Luke 2:36,37
** We meet him years later in Acts 3
*** We meet him years later in John 9

But back in her city in the hills of Judea, Elisabeth threw herself into her household duties and with helping others; politely listening to stories about children and now grandchildren, which most of her relatives and friends were having by now. By this time her childhood friend, Beth, who had had three daughters in four years during Elisabeth's and Zacharias' early marriage, was now a grandmother. Her two oldest daughters had married and her grandchildren numbered eleven from these two daughters. They lived close to Elisabeth, as well as their grandmother Beth, so Elisabeth heard about each birth, the milestones in their lives and really loved them because of her relationship to Beth. The children were all very special, and were often in Elisabeth's home.

There was Benjamin, (named after his father, who was at one time a Temple guard) a fourteen year old young man of faith, and handsome with dark eyes. He came close to death from an illness during his thirteenth year but the Lord, Who answers prayers, saved his life. Then came thirteen year old Caleb, who like the Caleb of old, *wholly followed the Lord.* [11] Next came Isaac, who had a heart for God even at nine years of age, and was full of life. Following him was the one girl in the family, Keturah, and she was seven, so sweet, had beautiful eyes and loved to sing praises to the Lord. Lastly came Mark, four years old, loving, active and always asking to pray at family prayer time. Their mother spent much time training the younger children, what time she was not involved with household chores and making garments. She was so skilled in making garments she could even make *a tunic without seam, woven top to bottom,*[12] a garment used by the priests.[13]

Beth's oldest daughter had two boys and four girls. Their father, Paul (very skilled in building), had a leadership role under Herod the Great in overseeing the repair of the Temple when he was much younger and single. Paul carefully trained his sons in his skills because he was fully aware that neglecting to teach his boys a craft for their future livelihood was perhaps teaching them to steal. There was thiteen year old Andrew, adept at learning the Scriptures and eager to follow in his father's footsteps. Then came lovely sensitive Anna, eleven years old, with a quiet deep faith in the Lord. Nine-year-old Daniel, who was named after Daniel, the prophet, followed her. Little Daniel loved to study bugs, lizards and brought them into their house to "study", much to the dismay of his mother! Rachael, just seven years old yet with a deep sensitivity to the Lord, was vivacious, with a smile that warmed every heart of those who saw her. Abigail, was only three but very animated and kept everyone in laughter. Sarah was only one year old but did her best to keep up with her older brothers and sisters. Their mother was even tempered in spite of her big brood and managed to have company over often. Their home was a hub of guests who sensed the welcome she and Paul afforded everyone who came there.

Beth loved her husband (a priest whom many Jews when ill sought out), grown daughters, sons-in-law, and grandchildren and spent as much time as she could with the grandchildren, knowing that before long they would be grown. Her love for her family, along with her love of nation, was only exceeded by her love for God.

Beth's youngest daughter, Miriam, did not marry until later in life but while she was home and single, she helped with her beloved nephews and nieces. Not only were they all devoted to her but so were the other children in the neighborhood. She would play games with them and could make them laugh at a moment's notice. *A merry heart does good like a medicine*[1 4] and her gift of joy was a balm for young and old alike. Miriam was even able to make Elisabeth laugh when the clouds of despair were heavy over her head.

Zacharias was occupied not only with his priestly obligations in Jerusalem but also with his duties in the synagogue in their city. And so the years passed but no matter how active they were, the husband and wife were always mindful of the shadow of Elisabeth's reproach. Aside from the loss of never having children to bless their home and to train as godly offspring, now they faced the specter of no adult children to care for them in their old age and that time was fast approaching.

They had fervently prayed together and individually for children but finally the time came when Elisabeth was past childbearing age. Since the way of women had ceased with her their prayers for a baby likewise ceased. After all, because of the circumstances, they knew it was too late for God to answer their prayers for children. Miraculous childbirth occurred in days of old but there were no reports of the Lord performing such miracles anymore. Neither could understand why the Lord had chosen to close Elisabeth's womb all these years but *in quietness and confidence*[15] they found strength, as they trusted the Lord. After all, who were they to question the sovereignty of God?

Chapter 4

A Heavenly Visitor

The Lord Breaks His 400 Years of Silence

And it came to pass, that while he executed the priest's office before God in the order of his course, according to the custom of the priest's office, his lot was to burn incense when he went into the temple of the Lord.
Luke 1:8,9

Early one afternoon Elisabeth was busy preparing Zacharias' favorite meal in anticipation of his return from his weeklong priestly ministry in Jerusalem. Over the years the couple had developed a little tradition upon his return from these trips. As soon as he was within hearing of the house he would call her name three times, unload and water his animal then enter the house. This signaled Elisabeth that he was back and gave her time to hurriedly wash her hands (because she was more than likely involved in kneading some dough or cleaning), replace straggling strands of gray hair, pat them in place, and straighten her robe. Having done all that she would quickly station herself by the door in preparation for a hearty hug and kiss.

But today was different. Although she thought she heard voices of the other priests she knew were traveling with Zacharias, she did not hear him call out her name. Instead, he burst through the door with a smile that stretched from ear to ear, visible even through his gray beard, and an excitement about him like she had never seen before! He hugged her and kissed her with tears of joy streaming down his cheeks and creating furrows in his travel dusty face. Elisabeth pleaded and exclaimed over and over, "Zacharias, what is going on? Tell me what this is all about! Why aren't you talking to me?" After many, almost comical gestures by Zacharias, (like a finger pointing to the heavens, then arms flapping at his sides to convey wings, and a finger pointing to his eyes), Elisabeth decided he wanted her to guess what they meant. She thought, "This seems like a game and so unlike my husband but I'll make a guess." Her conclusion from, 'something from the sky, with wings and he saw it' was blurted out in her first guess, "You saw a bird!" He irritatedly shook his head in the negative.

She thought again; something from the sky or heavens that flies, the only other thing she could think of was an angel so she asked half jokingly, "Did you see an angel?" He enthusiastically nodded in the affirmative. She thought, "How could this be true? The Lord has been silent for over four hundred years, why would He break His silence by sending an angel to speak to my husband?" Then Zacharias, to indicate what the angel had told him, made signs to her by placing his hands on Elisabeth's belly in a way to show it would grow. Next he folded his arms over his chest, one palm up as if cradling a baby and then placed the imaginary bundle into Elisabeth's arms.

This was too much for Elisabeth! It almost seemed as though this were some cruel joke but the joy and happiness on Zacharias' face stopped her short of expressing what she was thinking. Throughout the rest of the afternoon, by means of gestures and by writing on a tablet (for it was apparent for some reason Zacharias was not able to speak), Elisabeth pieced together what had happened during his time in Jerusalem.

It seems that it fell by lot for Zacharias to burn incense when he went into the Temple of the Lord. Elisabeth knew well the rituals of offering, like the morning and evening burnt offering of a male lamb one-year-old, without spot, which was offered with meat or flour and oil along with a drink offering of wine. She knew how the incense was then burned on the altar of incense before the morning sacrifice and after the evening sacrifice. She knew people would wait outside, pray and wait for the priest to bless them after the ceremony, for she had been part of that gathering many times. She knew this privilege of offering the incense was enjoyed only once in a priest's lifetime and some priests never participated in it because there were so many priests. What a joy for her husband to have been chosen for this highlight of his priesthood! He relayed the information about the multitude of people outside praying at that time and how he was praying and ministering at the altar while the sweet savor of incense ascended to the Lord.[1]

He related to her that during this time *there appeared unto him an angel of the Lord standing on the right side of the altar of incense.* Naturally, *when Zacharias saw him, he was troubled, and fear fell upon him. But the angel said unto him, "Fear not, Zacharias: for your prayer is heard, and your wife Elisabeth shall bear you a son, and you shall call his name John."*[2] At this point Elisabeth was beside herself in shock...their prayer had been heard! They had quit praying for a child years ago. Was the Lord answering their personal prayers that were prayed over and over for years even though they had stopped praying a decade or so ago? Or, had Zacharias been praying for Israel at the time of incense, as was the custom of most priests, and somehow we would have a child in answer to that prayer? Elisabeth could hardly take it all in! He interrupted her contemplation with more gestures and writing as the afternoon wore on and he communicated more to her about the angel's visitation and message to him.

She understood that the angel told him they would *have joy and gladness and many* would *rejoice at his birth.*[3] Elisabeth knew that must be an understatement of the joy she would sense to have a child, much less at her advanced age! The angel also said, *For he shall be great in the sight of the Lord, and shall drink neither wine nor strong drink.*[4] Elisabeth immediately recognized that their

A Heavenly Visitor

son would be under a lifetime Nazarite vow as were Samson and Samuel, whose mother had committed him to that vow during her prayers for a son. Next the angel told Zacharias that their son would *be filled with the Holy Spirit, even from his mother's womb.*[5] Oh, Elisabeth wondered, "How could this possibly be...all these promises, not only a son but that he would be filled with the Holy Spirit before he was born?" *And many of the children of Israel shall he turn to the Lord their God.*[6] Surely, this was more than anything for which they had prayed!

Then, wonder of wonders, the angel next said, *And he shall go before him in the spirit and power of Elijah, to turn the hearts of the fathers to the children, and the disobedient to the wisdom of the just; to make ready a people prepared for the Lord.*[7] Elisabeth could no longer keep silent. After four hundred years, the Lord HAD broken his silence to send an angel to her husband to announce that their son would be like Elijah for whom Israel had been looking for so long! And somehow he would be used to prepare the way for the Lord! The Lord had answered Zacharias' and Elisabeth's decades of prayers for a child, years after they had ceased praying. Elisabeth could no longer be silent but worshipped the Lord unashamedly crying out, "Blessed be the Holy One of Israel, all glory and honor to the One Who was and is and is to come!"

When Zacharias was able to get Elisabeth's attention again, he went on with his gestures and writing for there was more to make known to her regarding the angel's visitation. *And Zacharias said unto the angel, "Whereby shall I know this? For I am an old man, and my wife well stricken in years." And the angel answering him said, "I am Gabriel, that stand in the presence of God; and am sent to speak to you, and to show you these glad tidings. And behold, you shall be dumb and not able to speak, until the day that these things shall be performed, because you believed not my words, which shall be fulfilled in their season."*[8] Elisabeth finally understood why Zacharias could not speak. This was a warning to her not to doubt what had been promised to them but to trust that these things would come to pass no matter how impossible the circumstances seemed!

Her husband further conveyed to Elisabeth that *the people waited for Zacharias, and marvelled that he tarried so long in the temple* while he was offering incense. *And when he came out, he could not speak to them, and they perceived that he had seen a vision in the temple; and he beckoned to them and remained speechless. And it came to pass, that, as soon as the days of his ministration were accomplished, he departed to his own house.*[9] Poor Zacharias, he was so eager to return home and tell Elisabeth all that had happened but he had to remain in Jerusalem and finish his tour of duty even though he could not speak. Again, Elisabeth, with the news of the child to come, broke into praise to the Lord Who had been so gracious to all Israel and to their family!

For the first few weeks after that afternoon, joy abounded in their household. It could not be said that their life ever settled into routine after Zacharias returned home following the angelic visit. God had chosen to use this couple in a unique way and their lives would never be the same!

And after those days his wife Elisabeth conceived.[10] It had been a little over three months since Zacharias had returned home. A few mornings during that time she could not keep her breakfast down, a condition new to her but one she had often heard women experienced in early pregnancy. The way of women had ceased with her decades ago, so she did not have that as an indicator of pregnancy. Later she noticed her belly was beginning to swell ever so slightly. Could this be, did she possibly dare hope that this was the time spoken by the angel, Gabriel, when she would be with child?

And then, when she was four and a half months along and with a daily expanding waist, she felt her baby move within her. What joy! What delight! The Lord was surely bringing to pass the message Gabriel had given Zacharias. The Psalms of David had always been an inspiration to Elisabeth and his psalm concerning the unborn took on a new and personal meaning for her. *...You have covered me in my mother's womb, I will praise you; for I am fearfully and wonderfully made: marvellous are your works; and that my soul* knows right well. *My substance was not hid from you, when I was made in secret, and curiously wrought in the lowest parts of the earth. Your eyes did see my substance, yet being unperfect; and in your book all my members were written, which in continuance were fashioned, when as yet there was none of them.*[11] The Lord was fearfully and wonderfully forming her baby just as He does them all!

Elisabeth *hid herself* during this time, in fact for the first *five months* saying, *"Thus has the Lord dealt with me in the days wherein he looked on me, to take away my reproach among men."*[12]

And so the months passed after Zacharias returned. It was quieter around their home now than before extraordinary Zacharias' trip to Jerusalem because he still remained speechless. Oh, how he longed to be able to share with Elisabeth during this special time and to tell his friends and family the great news! But, he had to stand silently by while Elisabeth related the unbelievably good news of the angelic visitation and message.

Chapter 5
A Visitor with a Heavenly Message
Elisabeth has an Unexpected Visit from Mary

And Mary arose in those days, and went into the hill country with haste, into a city of Juda: And entered into the house of Zacharias, and saluted Elisabeth.
Luke 1:39,40

Elisabeth was well into the sixth month of pregnancy when she had an unexpected visit from her cousin, Mary, whom she and Zacharias loved and was now in her early teens. But the visit from the start was unlike any other. Mary, with much excitement in spite of the weariness from her weeklong journey, entered their house and greeted Elisabeth. *And it came to pass, that, when Elisabeth heard the salutation of Mary, the babe leaped in her womb; and Elisabeth was filled with the Holy Spirit: And she spoke out with a loud voice, and said, "Blessed are you among women, and blessed is the fruit of your womb, And what is this to me, that the mother of my Lord should come to me? For, lo, as soon as the voice of your salutation sounded in my ears, the babe leaped in my womb for joy. And blessed is she that believed: for there shall be a performance of those things that were told her from the Lord."*[1] Elisabeth instantly recalled Gabriel had told Zacharias their child would be filled with the Holy Spirit, even from his mother's womb and now, not only had her baby been filled but she was also filled with the Holy Spirit! Because of this filling, the Spirit had revealed to Elisabeth that Mary was "the mother of my Lord." While Elisabeth pondered this great truth, Mary, began to praise God melodiously saying:

> *My soul does magnify the Lord, and my spirit has rejoiced in God my Saviour.*[2]

"Ah," Elisabeth thought, "Mary, this special pure instrument chosen by God, knows that she, too, is a sinner like everyone else for *all have all sinned*[3] and she, too, needs a Savior. Mary's tender young mind had learned to worship the Lord but only her spirit could truly understand her salvation by God and speak forth in such a Holy Spirit revelation." Mary continued:

> *For he has regarded the low estate of his handmaiden: for, behold, from henceforth all generations shall call me blessed.*
> *For he that is mighty has done to me great things; and holy is his name.*
> *And his mercy is on them that fear him from generation to generation.*
> *He has shown strength with his arm; he has scattered the proud in the imagination of their hearts.*
> *He has put down the mighty from their seats, and exalted them of low degree.*
> *He has filled the hungry with good things; and the rich he has sent empty away.*
> *He has given help to his servant Israel, in remembrance of his mercy;*
> *As he spoke to our fathers, to Abraham, and to his seed forever.*[4]

"What a beautiful psalm!" exclaimed Elisabeth. "Who am I that I alone have heard this magnificent testimony? Would to God all His people could hear this!"

After Mary's resplendent psalm of praise, and when Elisabeth came back from her own worship of the Lord in her spirit, she questioned Mary about the reason for this glorious visit. What Mary had to say was even more marvelous and more miraculous than what had happened to Elisabeth and Zacharias over six months ago! Before she continued her story, Zacharias was summoned to see his beloved cousin, Mary, and to hear what the Lord had done in her life. While Elisabeth eagerly listened and sometimes asked questions for clarification, poor Zacharias could only listen. This is what Mary had to say:

Mary, who was *a virgin,* was *espoused to a man whose name was Joseph, of the house of David.*[5] A couple of weeks ago she was in her home in *a city of Galilee, named Nazareth,* north of Zacharias and Elisabeth's city in Judah, when Mary had a very unusual visitor… an angel! *The angel Gabriel was sent from God … and said to her, "Hail, you are highly favored, the Lord is with you: blessed are you among women."*[6] On hearing this, Zacharias immediately recognized the name of the angel who visited him! So did Elisabeth, but before she could say anything Mary went on:

And when she saw him, she was troubled at his saying, and cast in her mind what manner of salutation this should be. And the angel said to her, "Fear not, Mary: for you have found favor with God. And behold, you shall conceive in your womb, and bring forth a son, and shall call his name JESUS. He shall be great, and shall be called the Son of the Highest; and the Lord God shall give to Him the throne of His father David: and He shall reign over the house of Jacob forever; and of His kingdom there shall be no end." And Mary said to the angel, "How shall this be, since I know not a man?" And the angel answered and said to her, "The Holy Spirit shall come upon you, and the power of the Highest shall overshadow you: therefore also that holy thing which shall be born of you shall be called the Son of God."[7]

Elisabeth realized Mary, the beloved girl she and Zachariah had watched grow up, was that virgin who *would conceive.*[8] Elisabeth, in spite of being awestruck by this news, thanked the Lord that their dear cousin was that special one. Oh, the Lord's miraculous power and the depth and height of His love for His people!

After hearing what Mary had to say, Zacharias wrote the familiar Scripture on his tablet, *Therefore the Lord himself shall give you a sign, a virgin shall conceive, and bear a son, and shall call his name Immanuel,*[9] for Mary to see. Upon reading this scripture, Mary was awed and humbled as she realized this prophecy given hundreds of years ago was spoken of her.

When Mary gained her composure, she continued, and Elisabeth was brought back from her wonder when she heard that the angel had spoken her name, *"And behold, your cousin, Elisabeth, she has also conceived a son in her old age: and this is the sixth month with her who was called barren, For with God nothing shall be impossible." And Mary said, "Behold the handmaid of the Lord; be it unto me according to your word." And the angel departed from her.*[10] Gabriel's words to Mary, *For nothing will be impossible with God,* was a great truth spoken about Elisabeth's pregnancy in old age!

Mary's voice began to quiver and grew softer as she spoke of her dilemma after the angel left. The old couple, both with some hearing loss because of age, unconsciously leaned closer to be certain they heard every word. Mary related that after the angel departed she immediately wondered to whom she could go to share this marvelous news? Her first thought was her parents, but what would they think? What would they say? Would they believe her? Then, of course, her next thought was Joseph, but would he really understand? The only people she knew would understand were Zacharias and Elisabeth because the angel, Gabriel, told her that Elisabeth had conceived a son in her old age. "That's it!" she unconsciously blurted out. "I must see Zacharias and Elisabeth immediately!"

Mary knew the timing was not right to say anything to her parents about the angelic visitation but she needed to let them know her desire to see this older couple. Her parents thought the request for permission for the trip a little unusual but they knew of the mutual love Mary had with Zacharias and Elisabeth. They would agree to let her go if they could be assured of her safety on the trip. So arrangements were made as fast as possible. It was settled that Mary could make the trip with several relatives who were going in that direction with the next caravan of travelers. Her family was confident that she would be safe and helped her pack provisions, such as food and a warm robe to throw over her for those cold days and colder nights during this season. She would be sleeping out in the open and it would be cold.

Now after the weary week long trip of almost a hundred miles she was here in her cousins' warm familiar home, pouring her heart out to the only people she knew would understand. After she shared her good news, the three unashamedly wept with joy and spent much time in worship; Elisabeth and Mary were quite vocal but, alas, Zacharias still unable to speak, worshipped the Lord silently in his heart. After some time, Elisabeth shared with Mary the news of Zacharias' visit by Gabriel and the reason Zacharias could not speak. Mary rejoiced with them over the good news for not only their family but Israel, too. And so began the hours and hours of sharing what the Lord had done and was doing.

Chapter 6

Lord, Help Us Understand How We Fit into Your Plan

Mary Stays with Elisabeth for Three Months

I will meditate also of all thy work, and talk of thy doings.
Psalm 77:12

For three months Mary stayed with Elisabeth. They talked of the Lord, and His marvelous works, for many long hours, sometimes late into the night with a myriad of questions as to what all this meant. Sometimes Zacharias, upon overhearing their questions, would interject on his writing tablet some words of encouragement or understanding from the Scriptures. This interchange and time of searching was exactly what was needed by both women who were now central characters in this part of God's plan for the ages. Before this time, who would have thought that these two women; one an aged barren wife and the other a young engaged teen, would be so used by God?

Could they have known seven months before that God was sovereignly arranging history to use them? Now they carried in their wombs, sons who would change the course of history, (His story, God's story) in their lifetime, for years to come and for eternity! Surely, "God moves in mysterious ways His wonders to perform."[1] Who can know how God will *work all things together for good, to them that love God, to them who are the called according to his purpose?*[2] By His Holy Spirit within them, He was working greater things than either woman could have ever dared ask, think or imagined![3]

Often, during this time, Elisabeth could not sleep. Her sleeplessness was not only because of discomfort from her expanded belly, but also from the thoughts that flooded her mind regarding the supernatural events involving Zacharias, herself, and now Mary. Central to her thinking was that her son, John, would go before Mary's Son, Jesus, *in the spirit and power of Elijah.*[4] Then one night, as she was considering this, the thought of Elijah's cup she placed on the table when preparing the Passover meal came to mind. It suddenly dawned on her as she counted the months, that her son would be born about the time of Passover![5] What a fulfillment of prophecy! She could hardly wait to share this insight with Zacharias and Mary in the morning.

And that she did! But Zacharias had already entertained the identical thought and confirmed by gestures that he had come to the same conclusion. Mary, upon hearing this insight, began counting the months as to when her child would be born. She knew the Baby was conceived sometime in late December, so nine months from then would be around September and the Feast of Tabernacles! The Lord had dwelt in the Tabernacle in the wilderness and now He was dwelling in Mary. Surely, the Lord was by His attention to detail, working something, which was more than these three could comprehend at this time! But that caused them to seek Lord for even more revelation.

And so the time of Mary's visit passed quickly. Elisabeth's belly grew larger and larger yet she never tired of feeling her active unborn son move even when he disturbed her sleep. The Holy Spirit had *renewed Elisabeth's youth*[6] (as well as Zacharias') and *had quickened her mortal body*[7] so she could conceive and carry a baby. Even so, it was still awkward getting around to perform her usual household chores during the last months of her pregnancy. Then, too, when sleep eluded her because of her size and therefore did not feel very good the next day, she was especially grateful for Mary's help. Admittedly, Elisabeth, though she was thankful and excited to finally be pregnant, was also embarrassed because of her age.

As the time drew close for Mary to return home, she, herself, was beginning to experience a gentle swelling of her belly. It was just a week or so after she arrived at Elisabeth's home, she noticed the way of women had ceased with her so she knew that the Baby, conceived of the Spirit, was beginning to grow in her womb. But Mary had a very serious problem, which Elisabeth did not have. Elisabeth was married and even though the circumstances of her pregnancy were miraculous, no one would question who was the father of her child. For Mary it was quite different. She had never known a man and now she was returning to her hometown after several months away and returning obviously pregnant. What could she say? What would she say to her parents and most of all what would she say to dear Joseph who trusted her so completely? Surely he would assume she was pregnant by some man she had met on her trip. He knew it was not his child and the Law allowed him to have her stoned. Mary couldn't believe he would, inasmuch as he loved her, plus she had the promises given her by Gabriel for her future child, but Joseph could divorce her. Was that what would happen to her?

> *And Mary abode with her about three months, and returned to her own house.*
> Luke 1:56

"Oh, Zacharias and Elisabeth, please help!" she cried. They were the only people who knew the truth and believed what Mary had told them, but how could they help her? "Please, please," Mary cried, "Pray for me, for my family and most of all for Joseph and for the uncertainty the future holds for me!" And so, after three months in her cousins' home, arrangements were made for Mary to return home with some friends of the family in the next caravan of travelers. The return trip was more difficult; not knowing what to say to those in the caravan and not knowing what she had to face in Nazareth, but her visit with Zacharias and Elisabeth gave her understanding, encouragement and prayer support that would carry her through this time. Little did she know when she made this trip, that six months later, in the ninth month of pregnancy, she would be traveling almost the same long arduous journey.

Shortly after Mary left her cousins, the time of Passover arrived and Jews were celebrating the Feast. All devoted Jews were preparing to celebrate the Passover meal together and as usual, a place for Elijah was set at each table in anticipation of his arrival. And he did come, at least one who came in his spirit and power…as a baby now, and not the way that was expected.

Chapter 7
He Shall be Called John

Zacharias' and Elisabeth's Baby is Born

Now Elisabeth's full time came that she should be delivered; and she brought forth a son. And her neighbors and her cousins heard how the Lord had shown great mercy upon her; and they rejoiced with her. And it came to pass, that on the eighth day they came to circumcise the child; and they called him Zacharias, after the name of his father.
Luke 1:57-59

Elisabeth could not help but smile as she reflected on this centuries' old custom of neighbors coming at the time of circumcision to name the new baby. This could be traced back as far as the neighbors of Ruth, (wife of Boaz, and great grandmother to King David[1]) coming to name her baby and still the custom continued *And his mother,* Elisabeth, *answered and said, "Not so; but he shall be called John." And they said to her, "There is none of your kindred that is called by this name." And they made signs to his father, how he would have him called.*[2] Their friends and relatives had heard Zacharias could not speak and they assumed he could not hear either because all mutes with whom they were acquainted were deaf, too. So they signaled him, just as though he were deaf, to inquire about the child's name.

And he asked for a tablet, and wrote saying, "His name is John." And they marvelled all. And his mouth was opened immediately, and his tongue loosed, and he spoke, and praised God. And fear came on all that dwelt around them: and all these sayings were noised abroad throughout all the hill country of Judea. And all they that heard them laid them up in their hearts, saying, "What manner of child will this be!" And the hand of the Lord was with him.

And his father, Zacharias was filled with the Holy Spirit.[3] What a blessing, for after the baby had been filled in his mother's womb and Elisabeth was filled with the Spirit at Mary's greeting, now the father was also filled with the Holy Spirit. *And he prophesied, saying:*

> *"Blessed be the Lord God of Israel;*
> *for he has visited and redeemed his people,*
> *And has raised up an horn of salvation for us*
> *in the house of his servant David;*
> *As he spoke by the mouth of his holy prophets,*
> *which have been since the world began:*
> *That we should be saved from our enemies,*
> *and from the hand of all that hate us;*
> *To perform the mercy promised to our fathers,*
> *and to remember his holy covenant;*
> *The oath which he swore to our father Abraham,*
> *That he would grant unto us, that we being delivered out of the*
> *hand of our enemies might serve him without fear,*
> *In holiness and righteousness, before him,*
> *all the days of our life.*
> *And you, child, shall be called the prophet of the Highest:*
> *for you shall go before the face of the Lord to prepare his ways;*
> *To give knowledge of salvation unto his people*
> *by the remission of their sins,*
> *Through the tender mercy of our God;*

> *whereby the dayspring from on high has visited us,*
> *To give light to them that sit in darkness*
> *and in the shadow of death,*
> *To guide our feet into the way of peace."*[4]

What a blessing for Elisabeth to hear from her own husband's mouth that their son:

> would be called the prophet of the Most High,
> would go before the Lord to prepare His ways,
> to give to His people the knowledge of salvation
>   by the forgiveness of their sins,
>   through the tender mercy of our God.

Elisabeth had truly experienced the mercy of the Lord herself. Now she was a part of the deliverance to come to God's people through the One whose way would be prepared by their son. This was more than she could take in! Once again, Elisabeth, in her own way praised the Lord for His mighty acts, for what He had done in her life, and for what He was doing for Israel to fulfill promises He made centuries ago through the prophets.

As Elisabeth held her newborn close and nursed him, all the pain she experienced because of her empty years without children melted away. The Lord had heard their prayers and had not limited Himself to their finite view of circumstances. He had given them a testimony to His ways and power. She prayed and worshiped the Lord as she tenderly cared for and nourished her son, who, like all children, was a gift from God. This one was indeed a miraculous gift!

She thought of families celebrating Passover at this time and sending a child to the door to "hopefully welcome the prophet." Families who are hoping "that the prophet will step through the doorway, drink his cup of wine, and announce the coming of the Messiah."[5] *Elijah has already come, and they did not recognize him.*[6] If only Elisabeth could tell them so they would hear and believe,

"Yes, my child has come and you will one day see him *in the spirit and power of Elijah*,[7] as promised by the angel, and he will announce the coming of the Messiah!"

And the child grew, and waxed strong in spirit, and was in the deserts till the day of his showing unto Israel.

Luke 1:80

Chapter 8

But what About Mary?

She was Found with Child

> *When as his mother, Mary was espoused to Joseph, before they came together, she was found with child of the Holy Spirit.*
>
> Matthew 1:18

What was the reception she received after her weary return trip home to Nazareth? At first, when Joseph heard that Mary had returned, his heart was overjoyed! During her absence, this strong but gentle carpenter had worked on the house adjacent to his father's where he planned to take her after the wedding ceremony. Her inner beauty, her radiance, purity and obvious homemaking skills were the qualities which had drawn this righteous man to her with the desire to make her his wife. He was blessed beyond measure when she had happily consented to one day being his wife. He thought of their betrothal, arranged by his father, Jacob (named after the Jacob of old), the living patriarch of his family. How well he remembered that he and Mary enjoyed a joyous engagement celebration with relatives and friends less than a year ago.

Joseph had missed her presence in the village and the occasional glimpses of her while she was in Nazareth. He had been looking forward to her coming home but now was shocked and totally unprepared for the news he heard concerning her upon her return! He grieved beyond words and was in a state of unbelief when he heard the news, "Mary is expecting a Baby!" There was no way the Baby could be his! Question after question crowded his mind, "Mary is so pure, how could she do something like this?" "She knows this is sin and God will judge her, what happened?" "I thought we would be a godly family serving the Lord together with our future children and now...how could she disgrace my family and me like this?" "We were betrothed, there should have been no other man in her life, much less that she would have entered into a physical relationship with him!"

Joseph immediately sent his appointed friend of the bridegroom, who was the intermediary during this engagement period, to Mary's house for answers to Joseph's questions.[1] Mary explained in every detail the visit from Gabriel three months before and why she left so quickly to visit Zacharias and Elisabeth. But, "No," when Joseph was told, he did not comprehend any of this from what she said that her Baby was conceived of the Holy Spirit instead of some Roman soldier or some man she met on her travels. Finally, no matter how much she tried to explain, no matter how much she pleaded and no matter how much she cried, the word was sent back to her that Joseph could not understand.

And so the friend had to bear the bad news that she and Joseph must part; Mary, confused and in tears, and Joseph, numb from what was transpiring. What should he do? It seemed he had no choice. Certainly he would not have her stoned even though the Law allowed him to because of her unfaithfulness, as he supposed. He loved her too much in spite of what he thought she had obviously done. *Then Joseph, her husband* of the engagement year, *being a just man, and not willing to make her a public example, was minded to put her away privately.*[2] No matter how much he wanted to avoid it, he had to divorce her but he would do it quietly. There was no other way out.

And what about Mary? She was in turmoil. The night following their discussion through Joseph's friend was a sleepless night for her. Thoughts racing through her mind were Gabriel's words, along with the prayers and encouragement of Zacharias and Elisabeth, but her parents did not believe her, Joseph did not believe her and no one in their village believed her! How could she face the future with no human support? How could she rear this Child? "O, Lord, when You call someone to be used of You so mightily, man cannot perceive the call unless there is a revelation from You," she prayed. "Please make Joseph understand."

Because of Joseph's heavy heart sleep evaded him, until after hours of sleeplessness he finally fell into an uneasy slumber, planning how he would initiate a quiet divorce tomorrow. *But while he thought on these things, behold, the angel of the Lord appeared unto him in a dream, saying, "Joseph, thou son of David, fear not to take unto yourself Mary your wife: for that which is conceived in her is of the Holy Spirit. And she shall bring forth a son, and you shall call his name JESUS: for he shall save his people from their sins." Now all this was done, that it might be fulfilled which was spoken of the Lord by the prophet saying, "Behold, a virgin shall be with child, and shall bring forth a son, and they shall call his name, Emmanuel, which being interpreted is, God with us."*

Then Joseph being raised from sleep did as the angel of the Lord had bidden him.[3] He sent his friend to Mary's home at the first ray of early morning light. The words were delivered to Mary as though Joseph were there, "Mary, forgive me for not believing you! Surely, you know what happened to you is not something a man can grasp with his natural mind. It took an angelic visit in a dream for me to understand." Mary praised the Lord for sending an angel so Joseph would comprehend. She wept with joy over the revelation given him.

Gabriel had told both Joseph and Mary to name the Baby, JESUS. He told Joseph the reason being that He would save His people from their sin. Now Joseph, in this dream, had been told He would be called, Emmanuel, meaning "God with us." Mary remembered Gabriel's first greeting to her, *"Hail, you are highly favoured, the <u>Lord is with you</u>."*[4] In some measure, she was beginning to grasp how God was with her not only because of the miraculous conception, but also by the revelation to Joseph. Even so, she sensed this was just the beginning.

> *...And took unto him his wife: And knew her not till she had brought forth her firstborn son.*
> Matthew 1:24, 25

So, Joseph took Mary from her childhood home and after a quiet wedding ceremony she came to live in the home he had so painstakingly prepared. It was a little sparse in the way of furnishings; absent were the kind of furnishings and household items a couple normally receive as gifts during the wedding feast. The people who would have entered into the festivities of their wedding and brought gifts, instead looked with disdain upon Mary and Joseph because of her pregnancy during the engagement period. So, there was no usual celebration with friends and relatives for this couple. Mary had learned, and now Joseph was beginning to learn, too, that this Baby she was expecting would bring controversies and misunderstanding from now on.

A scantly furnished dwelling, friends and relatives who did not understand, and whispered ugly untrue rumors, were struggles for Mary. Joseph did his best to make up to her what they did not have in the way of material goods and to protect her from the ugly gossip, but she knew all too well what was being said. Joseph would hold her in his arms to comfort her but still, in a way, he kept his distance from her because he knew he was to keep her pure until after the birth of the Baby. God would give him the strength to do so and to meet his needs.

Joseph, now with the home finished and in anticipation of the Baby, applied his best carpentry skills to crafting a cradle for Him. Mary had been denied the festivities of a wedding ceremony but he would make it up to her in other ways; like making the best cradle ever made. He worked for weeks; first by acquiring just the right wood his meager income would allow, next by cutting the wood, working to make the wood smooth, fashioning it into a cradle. It was going to be something with which Mary would be pleased. They both admired the finished cradle and looked forward to the time they would lay Baby Jesus there.

As the weeks passed, Mary, at four and a half months of pregnancy, felt her unborn Son move for the first time. What joy! What excitement! Even the cruel remarks she had heard, almost daily from neighbors and others during her trips to the well and in the village, could not diminish this unique time. This new development and the evidential reality of the Baby soon to be born, again touched off a rash of questions between Mary and Joseph. When she first moved into their home they discussed with awe all day and late into many nights what could all this mean? Those discussions had somewhat subsided. Now with this unborn Baby's first felt movement their questions and wonders were renewed.

Oh! How they cherished the few sympathetic friends and relatives who withheld judgment regarding the Father of Mary's child. Most of Nazareth's population of about three hundred were from the Tribe of Judah and therefore expecting the Messiah to come through their tribe.[5] Yet, for the most part they were without insight regarding her Baby. However, an elderly man in their village, who was most knowledgeable regarding Messianic prophecies, began to put together familiar prophecies and recognized the fulfillment in events transpiring right in their little village. But still it was not so much, "This is the fulfillment," but more like, "Is it possible this could be the fulfillment?"

As the weeks passed, Mary's unborn Baby grew and so, too, her belly. It was getting more difficult to get around, especially in the last couple of months of her pregnancy. Joseph, always so attentive and caring for his wife, helped her as much as he could. Her Baby, like most unborn babies in this stage of growth, was very active at various times and Joseph, by placing his hand on her belly, could feel the unborn Baby's movements, too. Oh, the wonder of wonders of God's creation of these little ones! These were precious times when Mary and Joseph would unashamedly break forth in worship and praise to the Lord for His mercy to them and to all of Israel for this Promised Child.

Chapter 9

In the Fullness of Time

Mary Gives Birth

And it came to pass in those days, that there went out a decree from Caesar Augustus, that all the world should be taxed. (And this taxing was first made when Cyrenius was governor of Syria.) And all went to be taxed, every one into his own city.
Luke 2:1-3

During this time, Cyrenius became governor of Syria and Caesar Augustus was ruling from Rome. Mary and Joseph had resigned themselves to living under these oppressive rulers. They had not been touched significantly by civil government edicts up until now; although, like all Jews, they were looking for the time they would be out from under these oppressive Gentile rulers. However, there did come a ruling that would place an extreme hardship on them, especially Mary in her last month of pregnancy. A census had been decreed by Caesar Augustus and everyone had to return to his own city to be enrolled for taxing purposes. This could not have come at a worse time for the little family!

Mary was now in the ninth month of pregnancy and to make that weeklong trip over rugged terrain to Bethlehem would be extremely hard on her. What if the Baby was born during that trip, what would happen to her, to the Baby? Mary and Joseph were so poor they did not even have a donkey on which she could ride. But Mary, always filled with faith and cheer, encouraged Joseph and reminded him she had made a similar trip to see Zacharias and Elisabeth in late December when it was so cold. Certainly, she could make it now in September in better weather, even though she was nine months pregnant! Besides, she reminded Joseph, there would be plenty of travelers on the way to Jerusalem to celebrate the Feast of Tabernacles and surely someone would have pity on a wife, obviously expecting a baby at any moment, and allow her to ride on their donkey. "It would be a joyous trip" for the Jewish pilgrims flocking to Jerusalem for the Feast of Tabernacles, and there would be "much joy and singing on the way."[1] Mary and Joseph would be blessed to be part of the pilgrimage.

And so reluctantly, but with no other choice, Joseph made all the preparations and arrangements necessary for the journey. Mary, knowing that surely the Baby would be born before they returned, acquired some swaddling clothes in which to wrap her Baby, and some salt to clean the newborn, as was the custom.[2] She quietly tucked them with their other provisions for the trip.

Joseph's expressed concern that the trip would be extremely difficult for Mary was confirmed. Each time the company of travelers stopped for the night, Joseph carefully spread his cloak on the ground to make a soft warm bed for Mary. He next helped her off the donkey, one of the kind travelers had of-

And Joseph also went up from Galilee, out of the city of Nazareth, into Judea, unto the city of David, which is called Bethlehem; (because he was of the house and lineage of David) to be taxed with Mary his espoused wife, being great with child.

Luke 2:4,5

fered her, saw that she had some water and food and then she immediately fell into an exhausted sleep. It was usually some time before Joseph was finished with the duties of the day before he could prepare for sleep. At night, when sleep eluded him, he was drawn to the canopy of stars overhead, bright in the September sky. They seemed brighter than usual.

One night as he was partly praying and partly thinking about the numerous stars, he thought about the promise to Abraham that his descendents would be as numberless as the stars. Here Joseph and Mary, both being from the tribe of Judah, were descendents of that man of faith and therefore were two of the many numbers. Soon another star would be added. They were living in the land promised to Abraham but would they ever understand the fullness of the blessings promised for the world through Abraham's descendents? Joseph liked to meditate on such things for he seemed closer to God at those times and for a few minutes his mind was off his and Mary's own troubles. Joseph thought, "If a man can trust God like Abraham, even when he can not see things as God does, he will have the faith to face anything, fully confident that God is in control." With those words firmly fixed in his heart, he slowly drifted off to sleep.

After daybreak and after he and Mary had eaten something from their provisions, he helped Mary up onto the donkey, then they and the other travelers started out again. Having a donkey on which to ride was such a blessing for her. That eased her discomfort somewhat but by the time they reached Bethlehem she was exhausted and beginning to sense pains in her belly. She didn't have to say anything to Joseph nor to some observant women traveling with them because they all could read her face when she quietly winced with beginning birth pangs. Because of the rigors of such a hard journey, it was a miracle that she didn't give birth on the long trip!

Joseph knew time was short and he must not only find her a place suitable to birth the Baby but a woman to help with the delivery! However, the people coming for the census and travel-

> *...because there was no room for them in the inn.*
> Luke 2:7

ers on their way to Jerusalem to celebrate the Feast of Tabernacles crowded the city. Through throngs of people, Joseph with Mary went from inn to inn looking for a place to stay. Finally, the last innkeeper from whom he sought lodging, saw the couple and sized up the situation but having no room (or possibly not wanting to make room since he didn't want his guests disturbed by a woman giving birth) suggested another place.

Close by there was a stable, a part of a cave, often used by the shepherds, who tend the flocks bred for offerings for the Temple. There they would bring their ewes who were birthing lambs and needed a shelter from bad weather.[3] It was maintained clean and Joseph and Mary could go there. It was not too far from the inn. Joseph gratefully accepted the offer and the offer of a lamp given him by the innkeeper, then hurried Mary to the stable. On the way, he passed a woman, who had befriended them during their travels and who had not only helped with other births, but had offered Mary help when her time came. The woman instantly recognized the signs and joined the couple, knowing the Baby's birth would be soon.

Joseph gently lifted Mary from the donkey and placed her on the clean straw he had quickly arranged for her. As fast as he could he found some water for her to drink and arranged for her to be as comfortable as possible because he knew, as well as the acting midwife[4], the birth was eminent!

Since men did not help with birthing of babies, Joseph obviously had no experience assisting a woman giving birth. However, any little thing Mary asked from him was quickly done. Joseph couldn't help but think, "All Mary has been through and now this; a midwife she's only

> *And so it was that, while they were there, the days were accomplished that she should be delivered.*
> Luke 2:6

known a short time to help her, an awkward and somewhat embarrassed husband who must step out and let the midwife handle the birth. Not only that, they were miles away from relatives and friends who would normally be here to help and to rejoice with her." It had certainly had been a difficult time for both of them!

In a short time, the Baby was born. Mary, with hair damp from perspiration during labor, was exhausted but so pleased when the midwife handed her the Baby after cutting the umbilical cord and cleaning Him up by rubbing salt on Him. In the meantime, Joseph had located the swaddling clothes among their provisions, and Mary gently wrapped her Precious Bundle in them. Next she tenderly placed her Baby to her breast to receive His first nourishment. The midwife, having finished her duties, departed amidst a profusion of grateful words from the appreciative couple.

And she brought forth her firstborn son, and wrapped Him in swaddling clothes...
Luke 2:7

By the dim light of the lamp Mary and Joseph studied the Baby's delicate facial features, His tiny hands, fingers, and toes then gently kissed His face. How awed they were of this Little One. Unconsciously Mary and then Joseph began to speak in wonder and adoration the names Gabriel told them this Holy Child would be called and now engraved on Mary and Joseph's hearts: "Jesus, Son of the Most High, Son of God, and Emmanuel, 'God with us'." They both, without saying a word, knew they were looking into the eyes of God, yes, they were seeing Him face to face. What more could be said but in quietness try to absorb this Wonder of Wonders.

Silent night, holy night!
All is calm, all is bright,
Round yon virgin mother and Child,
Holy Infant so tender and mild;
Sleep in heavenly peace
Sleep in heavenly peace.

Silent night, Holy night!
Son of God, Love's pure light.
Radiant beams from Thy Holy Face
With the dawn of redeeming grace,
Jesus Lord at Thy birth,
Jesus Lord at Thy birth.[5]

...laid Him in a manger.
Luke 2:7

When the Newborn had finished nursing, Mary needed to find a place to lay Him because she required some rest herself. Joseph quickly surveyed their surroundings and spied a manger. He freshened it up with clean straw for a bed for the Little One. Mary then carefully laid Him in the manger as she prepared to take a rest.

Unknown to Mary and Joseph, all the host of heaven was rejoicing at this time because of this expression of the Father's love for the world in giving His only Begotten Son![6] Obviously, during the birth neither Mary nor Joseph could give the significance of this birth its rightful notice but all of heaven was abounding with attention and exultation because of God's Gift of Love! Joy of the angels was unrestrained and not even heaven could retain it all! Mary and Joseph would soon learn whom God had chosen to have a glimpse of the boundless heavenly worship and to hear the Good News.

> Away in the manger, no crib for a bed,
> The Little Lord Jesus laid down His sweet head;
> The stars in the sky looked down where He lay;
> The little Lord Jesus asleep in the hay.[7]

Joseph thought about the little finely crafted cradle in their home in Nazareth that would remain empty for who knows how long. Somehow, all the provisions Joseph had planned for Mary when he first decided to marry her; like a festive wedding feast with guests, gifts, and blessings, had not materialized because of her misunderstood pregnancy. Now she suffered the absence of her family and friends to share in the joy of her Firstborn. She didn't even have a decent place to birth the Child nor a cradle in which to lay Him. Yes, Mary had given up much to be this special mother. Joseph, too, had suffered the loss of being able to provide for his family in a way that he wanted. He learned that sometimes the provisions a man plans for his family may not materialize because of circumstances but he was fast learning he must trust God no matter what happens.

Chapter 10
Shepherds Seek the Lamb

Angels Announce the Baby's Birth to Shepherds

And there were in the same country shepherds abiding in the field, keeping watch over their flock by night.
Luke 2:8

Voices of men brought Joseph back from his reverie. Mary had been so sleepy, but before she could close her eyes, she and Joseph both heard men talking just outside. "Who is that?" she asked Joseph. He nodded his head and shrugged his shoulders in a way as to indicate he did not know but would find out. He moved quickly in the direction of the voices and upon seeing the men, whom he recognized to be shepherds, asked them if something was wrong. Joseph was amazed at the words which tumbled from their lips. After hearing just a few words, Joseph knew Mary must hear them, too. He motioned for the men to come in before continuing and asked them to tell his wife what they had told him and then finish telling the whole story of the reason for their visit. Joseph ushered the shepherds ahead of him into the stable but before Joseph came in, he noticed a very bright star in the sky directly over the stable, which he had not seen when they first came to the stable.

These weather worn shepherds started first toward Mary until their eyes adjusted to the soft light of the lamp, and then they saw the Babe in the manger. Their eyes reverently gazed instead at the Little One. When they approached the manger, with the Baby lying there wrapped in swaddling clothes, they all dropped to their knees at once in humble adoration repeating in tones of worship the names, "Savior" and "Christ the Lord." Mary still did not understand. It was as though these men knew all about the angelic visits to her and Joseph and the names and promises given them for the Baby! Yet she knew Joseph had not had time to tell them.

Joseph withheld his questions so as to avoid interrupting the shepherds' worship. When it subsided, Joseph asked them again if they would be so kind as to tell his wife what they had briefly told him outside the stable. First one explained they were shepherds who watched over the flock of sheep bred for offerings in the Temple at Jerusalem. In fact, another shepherd added that they often brought their ewe lambs to this very stable to give birth since it was part of a cave and the ewes would be protected. The first shepherd then described what happened on this most unusual night:

And there were in the same country shepherds abiding in the field, keeping watch over their flock by night. Just a short time ago, *the angel of the Lord came upon them, and the glory of the Lord shown round about them: and they were sore afraid.*[1] One of the shepherds, previously silent, pleaded with Mary and Joseph not to think of them as cowards for being frightened at the sight of an angel. He assured them that if they ever saw an angel they would be frightened, too! Mary quickly bowed her head hoping to hide a faint smile while exchanging knowing glances with Joseph, who, with his hand, was making an unsuccessful attempt at hiding a more obvious amused smile. Both went unnoticed by the shepherds in the dim light, and neither said a word while the shepherd continued.

And the angel said unto them, "Fear not: for, behold, I bring you good tidings of great joy, which shall be to all the people. For unto you is born this day in the city of David a Savior, which is Christ the Lord. And this shall be a sign unto you; you shall find the babe wrapped in swaddling clothes, lying in a manger."[2] Mary was amazed! The circumstances had dictated a manger for a cradle, or though it seemed the circumstances dictated, but the Lord was orchestrating everything for the birth of this Baby...even to His swaddling clothes and His lying in a manger as a sign to the shepherds!

The shepherd, who had taken the role of spokesman, continued the story of their angelic visit: About the time the shepherds had recovered from the shock of seeing one angel and then trying to absorb what was said, they were visited again; this time by a multitude of angels without number which filled the heavens! For *suddenly there was with the angel a multitude of the heavenly host praising God, and saying, "Glory to God in the highest, and on earth peace, good will toward men."*[3] It was difficult to understand the shepherds after this piece of information was related because everyone of them began talking at once about the beauty of the night sky that had been filled with angels proclaiming praises to God.

> Hark! The herald angels bring,
> "Glory to the newborn King.
> Peace on earth and mercy mild,
> God and sinners reconciled!"
> Joyful, all ye nations, rise;
> Join the triumph of the skies;
> With th'angelic host proclaim,
> Christ is born in Bethlehem![4]

One by one, the shepherds related more of their story. *And it came to pass, as the angels were gone away from them into heaven, the shepherds said one to another, "Let us now go even unto Bethlehem, and see this thing which has come to pass which the Lord has made known to us."*[5] They knew they had to act on the message so they quickly drew lots to determine which shepherds would stay to tend the flock and who would go. *And they came with haste, and found Mary, and Joseph, and the babe lying in the manger.*[6]

Joseph asked the shepherds if they knew why this announcement would be made to them? They did not. They were stunned themselves and questioned each other as to the meaning of this angelic announcement, much less why it would be made to these shepherds of the special sheep for Temple offerings. They did not know why but they did know they were blessed beyond words that God had sovereignly chosen them to see the Baby, Who is Christ the Lord.

After some time the shepherds reluctantly said good-by to the blessed couple but departed with praises on their lips for the Christ Child, the Holy Babe. After they left they *made known abroad the saying which was told them concerning this child. And all they that heard it wondered at those things which were told them by the shepherds. But Mary kept all these things and pondered them in her heart. And the shepherds returned, glorifying and praising God for all the things that they had heard and seen, as it was told unto them.*[7]

Soon after the shepherds' departure, Mary fell into a much-deserved but short sleep. She was all too soon awakened by the hungry cry of her Newborn, Who not only needed feeding but also a change of His swaddling clothes. Joseph carried Him from the manger to Mary, who after changing Him drew Him close to her side and nursed Him until they both fell asleep.

Joseph, unable to fall asleep right away because of the excitement of the Baby's birth and visit by the shepherds, glanced around their surroundings dimly lit by the moon and new bright star. The thought came to him of how much being in this stable and out of a house, reminded him of the booths in which other Jews, celebrating the Feast of Tabernacle, were staying at this time. During this time Jews had left their homes to live in temporary dwellings they prepared as a reminder of their ancestors' wilderness wandering after they had left Egypt under Moses centuries ago. Now, in a way God, Himself, had left His home to live in a temporary dwelling He had prepared. Joseph did not spend too much time in thought before he drifted off into a weary sleep, too. *And the Word was God…and the Word was made flesh and dwelt* [tabernacled] *among us.*[8]

Yea, Lord, we greet Thee, Born this happy morning:
Jesus, to Thee be all glory given;
Word of the Father, Now in flesh appearing;
O Come let us adore Him, O come let us adore Him,
O Come let us adore Him, Christ the Lord.[9]

Christ, by highest heaven adored; Christ, the everlasting Lord!
Late in time behold Him come,
Off-spring of the virgin's womb:
Veiled in flesh the Godhead see; Hail the incarnate Deity;
Pleased as Man with men to dwell, Jesus, our Immanuel!

Hail, the heaven-born Prince of Peace! Hail,
the Sun of Righteousness!
Light and life to all He brings,
Rise'n with healing in His wings.
Mild He lays His glory by, Born that man no more may die,
Born to raise the sons of earth, Born to give them second birth.

Come Desire of Nations, come,
Fix in us Thy humble home.
Rise the woman's conq'ring Seed,
Bruise in us the serpents' head,
Adam's likeness now efface, Stamp Thine image in its place
Second Adam from above, Reinstate in us Thy love.[10]

Chapter 11

Circumcision of the Baby

His Name was Called JESUS

And when eight days were accomplished for the circumcising of the child, his name was called JESUS...
Luke 2:21

The days following the Baby's birth were days of adjustment. Mary was blessed in her maternal role and gained strength back in a short time. Even though Joseph was with Mary and the Baby to help as much as possible, he did have to leave for various reasons. He had to find provisions, to take care of the census business and be in Jerusalem just a few miles away for the Feast celebration but was at her side whenever he could be there.

The days since the birth had passed quickly even though their living quarters had been out of the ordinary, to say the least. Mary had already adjusted to the Baby's required feedings every few hours all day and through the night, plus His necessary changes in clothes. Keeping His swaddling clothes clean had been a challenge. There was no point in returning to Nazareth now because Joseph and Mary would have to be in Jerusalem for her purification offering in about five weeks.

The stable was an unusual dwelling for the Infant's first week. On the evening of the seventh day, the innkeeper offered the couple a house in which to stay. The house belonged to a friend of his who had traveled to another town for awhile. The friend had instructed the innkeeper to keep an eye on it because he and his family would be gone for quite sometime. Another family visiting in Bethlehem for the census and their daily trips to Jerusalem for the Feast of Tabernacles was leaving today now that the Feast was nearing completion. Surely, the innkeeper concluded, his friend who owned the house would not mind if he allowed this needy couple to stay there.

Joseph eagerly accepted the offer and gathered up their meager belongings in preparation for the move while Mary gently lifted the Baby from His place in the manger, which had been His most unusual bed. They now had a little house in which to live while they waited for the fortieth day of her purification in the Temple. So they settled down in this temporary home.

That first night in the little house, after Mary and the Baby were asleep, Joseph noticed through the windows the stars in the sky again. He wondered what had happened to the new bright star that he had seen over the stable where they had been living. Quietly stepping out of the house for a better look, he saw that it now appeared to be directly over their house!

And when eight days were accomplished for the circumcising of the child, his name was called JESUS, which was so named of the angel before he was conceived in the womb.
— Luke 2:21

Joseph had found a priest in Jerusalem to circumcise the Baby and on the eighth day after His birth, in accordance with the Law of Moses, He was circumcised. At that time they named Him, JESUS, in obedience to the instructions given them by the angel, Gabriel. This was a time of much joy! Being the 8th day of the Feast of Tabernacles this was the time of

"Rejoicing of Finishing the Law." Last night, being the evening of the 7th day was "Rejoicing in the Law" and the time when all the Jews moved back into their houses. This morning had been the celebration of the "Bridegroom of the Law." Mary and Joseph's joy over Jesus' circumcision and His being named, were mingled with exultation associated with the Feasts.[1]

While they were waiting for the end of forty days, Joseph found little carpentry jobs here and there to bring in some income. Even so, it was a meager income and the jobs were more difficult without his own tools. They mistakenly thought they were settling into a routine of daily living as they reviewed the miraculous events that had transpired in the past few months but, little did they know, there were more to come.

Joseph considered all that had transpired in just a few short months. He would meditate on these things; especially, at night when he would step out of the little home to leave Mary and the Baby so he could be alone with God and pray. He wasn't outside long, however, before his attention was drawn from past events to the intriguing bright star that stayed directly over the house. Did the star have some significance? So many unusual events had happened to them already, he decided it must have something to do with Jesus' birth but he did not know what.

Chapter 12
Presentation in the Temple

Simeon and Anna Bless the Baby

And when the days of her purification according to the law of Moses were accomplished, they brought him to Jerusalem, to present him to the Lord... and to offer a sacrifice... a pair of turtledoves or two pigeons.
Luke 2:22, 24

On the fortieth day after Jesus' birth, Mary and Joseph traveled the familiar five miles to Jerusalem to offer sacrifices for her purification. As usual the streets of the city bustled with merchants, shoppers, travelers and the country dwellers coming to the city along with the usual city dwellers. However, it was nothing to equal the activity during the days of the three Feasts when all Jewish men were required to be in Jerusalem! Joseph secured the pair of turtledoves necessary for sacrifice and their cooing went unnoticed by the Babe sleeping so peacefully in His mother's arms.

And, behold, there was a man in Jerusalem, whose name was Simeon; and the same man was just and devout, waiting for the consolation of Israel: and the Holy Spirit was upon him. And it was revealed unto him by the Holy Spirit, that he should not see death, before he had seen the Lord's Christ. And he came by the Spirit into the temple: and when the parents brought in the child Jesus, to do for him after the custom of the law, Then he took him up in his arms, and blessed God, and said, "Lord, now let your servant depart in peace, according to your word: For my eyes have seen your salvation, Which you have prepared before the face of all people; A light to lighten the Gentiles, and the glory of your people Israel."

And Joseph and his mother marvelled at those things which were spoken of him.[1] Joseph and Mary were amazed, first with all the angel and the shepherds had told them regarding her Son and now this. Joseph was overwhelmed with the realization that only the Lord could direct them as to how to rear and care for His Holy Child. During their consideration of these matters, Simeon spoke again,

And Simeon blessed them, and said unto Mary his mother, "Behold, this child is set for the fall and rising again of many in Israel; and for a sign which shall be spoken against; (Yea, a sword shall pierce through your own soul also,) that the thoughts of many hearts may be revealed."[2] This greatly disturbed Mary! What could this possibly mean "that a sword would pierce her own soul?" Why not Joseph's soul, too? Simeon, tenderly and reverently placed the Babe back into Mary's arms and departed from them worshipping and praising the Lord.

Joseph and Mary, preparing to go into the Temple area, were still in deep discussion regarding what Simeon had said when they were approached by a very thin, almost gaunt old woman bent over with age. *And there was one Anna, a prophetess, the daughter of Phanuel, of the tribe of Aser, she was of great age, and had lived with an husband seven years from her virginity; And she was a widow of about fourscore and four years, which departed not from the temple, but served God with fastings and prayers night and day. And she coming in that instant gave thanks likewise unto the Lord, and spoke of him to all them that looked for the redemption in Jerusalem.*[3] Anna, too, had received a revelation of Who this Child was! Mary and Joseph both were attentive to all she said about the Child and Mary pondered all these things in her heart.

They returned to Bethlehem to take up residence again but this time to begin enjoying their husband and wife relationship, a blessing given by the Lord, now *that she had brought forth her firstborn son.*[4] They settled down in the temporary house, believing the Lord would give them clear directions concerning when to leave Bethlehem and return to Nazareth.

Chapter 13

A Star in the East

A Visit from the Wise Men

Where is he that is born King of the Jews? For we have seen his star in the east, and are come to worship him.

Matthew 2:2

Some time after the small family returned to Bethlehem, they again had visitors…even more unusual than the shepherds! This time it was wise men, visitors from the East, learned men with an impressive retinue of servants. By the time the men had dismounted from the camels, their servants had located the valuable gifts brought from their country for the newly born King of Jews and placed them into the hands of the wise men. They reverently entered the house a*nd when they were come into the house, they saw the young child with Mary His mother; and fell down and worshiped Him: and when they had opened their treasures, they presented unto Him gifts; gold, and frankincense and myrrh.*[1] What gifts these men lavished on the Baby! There was gold, so often symbolic of a king. Did not Gabriel tell Mary that her Son shall be given *the throne of his father David and he will reign over the house of Jacob for ever; and of his kingdom there will be no end?*[2] And frankincense, symbolic of the priesthood and the offering of incense, and lastly, myrrh, symbolic of a prophet or could this be the embalming spice that symbolized death. Mary shuddered as she remembered Simeon's words, *Yea, a sword shall pierce through thy own soul also.*[3] Did the myrrh have any connection to his words?

> Gold I bring to crown Him again,
> King forever, ceasing never,
> Over us all to reign.
> Born a King on Bethlehem's plain,
>
> Frankincense to offer have I;
> Incense owns a Deity nigh.
> Prayer and praising, all men raising,
> Worship Him, God most high.
>
> Myrrh is mine, its bitter perfume
> Breathes a life of gathering gloom,
> Sorrow, sighing, bleeding, dying,
> Sealed in the stone cold tomb.[4]

But Joseph and Mary were still mystified how these men knew where they were and who told them about the deity of this Child. After the gifts were presented and after sufficient time had lapsed for these noble travelers, along with their retinue, to worship the Object of their devotion, Joseph kindly asked them to explain their presence. This is what was told the couple: "We are from the Land of the East, from Babylon, and are descendants of the Jews who were brought into captivity there centuries ago but did not return to the land of Israel when they were allowed to go.[5] We have been studying the scrolls brought there by our captured ancestors and are seeking the One Whom God in His Holy Word promised to send. We study the stars and when we saw His star in the East we knew we must follow it to see Him. We followed the star to Jerusalem but then we no longer saw it. When we had arrived in Jerusalem, we asked around the city, "*Where is he that is born King of the Jews? For we have seen his star in the east, and are come to worship him.*"[6] Mary and Joseph were a little surprised that the shepherd's news of the Baby, extensively broadcast around, had not reached Jerusalem.

The news of the wise men's inquiry eventually reached Herod's ears. *And when Herod the king had heard these things, he was troubled, and all Jerusalem with him.*[7] Is it any wonder that this power crazed king, who had been given the title, King of the Jews, by the Roman Senate under Emperor Caesar Augustus[8] would be troubled at the announcement of another King of the Jews born just five miles from his throne? Surely the people would be concerned, too, because they had no idea what turmoil lay ahead if these two kings eventually fought it out for the throne.

Herod knew he must question the Jewish religious leaders who could explain the prophecies and so he called them in. *And when he had gathered all the chief priests and scribes of the people together, he demanded of them where Christ should be born. And they said unto him, In Beth-lehem of Judaea: for thus it is written by the prophet, "And thou Bethlehem, in the land of Juda, art not the least among the princes of Juda: for out of thee shall come a Governor, that shall rule my people Israel."*[9]

The wise man who had been speaking, hesitated, licked his dry lips and then continued. "Now that Herod knew where the child would be born, *he privately called the wise men, inquired of them diligently what time the star appeared. And he sent them to Bethlehem, and said, 'Go and search diligently for the young child; and when you have found him, bring me word again, that I may come and worship him also.' When they had heard the king, they departed; and, lo, the star, which they saw in the east, went before them, till it came and stood over where the young child was.*[10] As we mentioned, for some reason we did not see the star for awhile but when we left Jerusalem it appeared again. *When* we *saw the star, we rejoiced with exceeding great joy.*"[11] Now Mary and Joseph at last knew why these men were in the house, why they were worshiping the Newborn and why the bright star shown first over the stable and now the house!

> They looked up and saw a star
> Shining in the East beyond them far,
> And to the earth it gave great light,
> Noel, Noel, born is the King of Israel.[12]

The wise men had learned of the prophecy concerning the Child's birth in Bethlehem of Judea from the religious leaders in Jerusalem. Joseph, being reminded of that prophecy, remembered the many prophecies concerning the Baby, which had been fulfilled in such a short time. Surely, only One Who is God, can fulfill prophecy by arranging the circumstances of His own birth!

After the wise men were given sufficient time to hold the Holy Child and worship Him, they and their company departed from Mary and Joseph. They had every intention of returning to tell Herod of their find so that he, too, could worship the Child. Because the men were from a foreign land they did not know just how wicked Herod was or they would never have believed he really wanted to worship the Child. During the first night after visiting the Christ Child, the wise men were *warned of God in a dream they should not to return to Herod, they departed for their own country by another way.*

And when they were departed, behold, the angel of the Lord, appeared to Joseph in a dream, saying, "Arise, and take the young child and his mother, and flee into Egypt, and be there until I bring you word: for Herod will seek the young child to destroy him." When he arose, he took the young child and his mother by night, and departed into Egypt. [13]

The little family lost no time in gathering their belongings, including gifts from the wise men, and left by night lest they be seen and joined a caravan traveling in the direction of Egypt. Mary was not accustomed to traveling with the Little One so it was especially difficult. Could that wicked Herod have stationed his soldiers along Mary and Joseph's route to Egypt? Was it necessary to keep the child quiet? She probably nursed Him more than He needed just to be sure He would not be heard. Mary thought of Jocabed, Moses' mother, who must have nursed him more than needed in order to keep him quiet and hidden from Pharoah's men. The Lord providentially used the very government planning baby Moses' destruction as the instrument for his protection. That encouraged her, plus all the promises given Mary and Joseph regarding the Child. God would take care of them and preserve His life just as He had Moses in the basket.

Then Herod, when he saw that he was mocked of the wise men, was exceeding angry, and sent forth, and slew all the children that were in Bethlehem, and in all the coasts thereof, from two years old and under, according to the time which he had diligently inquired of the wise men.[14] Herod had carefully calculated the time. He knew that it had taken some time for the wise men to study the star they had discovered at the time of the Baby's birth. Besides, it took more time to decide to seek this King of Jews and to make arrangements for their travels plus the time to travel the long distance with their great company. With Herod's reckoning of age from the time of conception so the Baby was already considered nine months old when He was born, is it any wonder he included all male babies two years old and below?[15] Herod wanted to be sure he killed the One Who was a supposed threat to his throne.

Then was fulfilled that which was spoken by Jeremy the Prophet, saying, "In Rama, was there a voice heard, lamentation, and weeping, and great mourning, Rachel weeping for her children, and would not be comforted, because they are not."

Matthew 2:17-18

When Mary heard of Herod's murderous atrocities of these innocent children, she was moved to think that these little ones, in some special way, had given their lives for her Baby. Mary prayed for those mothers who had lost their children to this ruling madman. She thought of Elisabeth and her son, John, who was of the age of children Herod ordered killed. She prayed that Herod's edict would not reach their city so that the child, John, would be spared. Surely, the Lord will not hold this man guiltless for this must be the most heinous act of all Herod's commands… the deliberate murder of innocent babies because they might get in his way...the way of his throne. It was all a diabolical plan instigated and driven by Satan himself through his instrument, Herod!

At first there was some anxiety on the couple's part regarding how to obtain provisions they needed for their journey. Certainly, Joseph being away from his carpentry shop had only done little jobs here and there since they left Nazareth. Their limited income had been sorely strained. But they remembered the gifts given by the wise men and knew by the sale of these as needed there would be enough to supply all their needs. God had once again shown Himself as Jehovah-Jireh, the One Who looks ahead and provides.[16]

Before long, Herod, who had been ill and in painful distress for some time, died. Was his death a judgment of God for his orders for the murder of innocent babies? *God is not mocked: for whatsoever a man sows, that shall he also reap.*[17]

But when Herod was dead, behold, an angel of the Lord appeared in a dream to Joseph in Egypt, saying, "Arise, and take the young child and his mother, and go into the land of Israel: for they are dead which sought the young child's life." And he arose, and took the young child and his mother and came into the land of Israel.[18]

Chapter 14

Home at Last

He Shall be Called a Nazarene

And he came and dwelt in a city called Nazareth: that it might be fulfilled which was spoken by the prophets, He shall be called a Nazarene.
Matthew 2:23

But when he heard that Archelaus did reign in Judaea in the place of his father Herod, he was afraid to go there: notwithstanding, being warned of God in a dream he turned aside into the parts of Galilee.[1] to their own city Nazareth.[2] Mary was so thankful for the guidance the Lord had given Joseph. This was the fourth time Joseph had miraculously received direction in a dream. The Lord had been so merciful to lead Joseph in dreams so this Child would be safe. Mary thought, surely, there will come a day when we can settle down and begin what she longed for, what might be considered a normal life back in their hometown of Nazareth. But then again she concluded, what could be considered normal about rearing the Son of God?

Home at last! Now Mary could place Jesus in that special cradle lovingly made by Joseph months ago; although, it seemed more like decades ago. So much had happened to them since they left Nazareth when Mary was in her ninth month of pregnancy: miles of travel, birthing the Baby in a stable, supernatural visitations in dreams, angelic proclamations, visitations by shepherds, blessings by Simeon and Anna in the Temple, a star over their house, visitations by wise men, children murdered, and travel, travel, travel. It would take a lifetime for Mary and Joseph to weave all this together for any kind of understanding even if that was possible in this life. But for now, she was ready to settle down with Joseph, and rear the Promised Child, the Son of God and look forward to other children, Joseph's children, who would in time be added to their family. Joseph was already talking about naming one of his sons, James.[3]

They did not know the future but they trusted the One Who directs and controls the future.

And the child grew, and waxed strong in spirit, filled with wisdom: and the grace of God was upon him.

Luke 2:40

*For unto us a child is born, unto us a son is given:
and the government shall be upon his shoulder:
and his name shall be called Wonderful,
Counsellor, The mighty God,
The everlasting Father, The Prince of Peace.
Of the increase of his government
and peace there shall be no end,
upon the throne of David, and upon his kingdom,
to order it, and to establish it with judgment
and with justice from henceforth even for ever.
The zeal of the LORD of Hosts will perform this.*

Isaiah 9:6-7

(Readers are encouraged to turn to Appendix D where Bible verses used in this text are given without story line or comments, except for section titles. It is important to leave this reading with a clear understanding of what the Word of God actually says about these births and what has been presented in this book as the author's comments.)

Endnotes

Chapter 1 Memories of Better Times

1. *Manners & Customs of the Bible* by James M. Freeman, Logos International, Plainfield, NJ, reprinted 1972, p. 403.
2. Ibid. p. 330.
3. Ibid. p. 423.
4. John 14:3.
5. *"That the World May Know"* series, *Faith Lession 14: No Greater Love / Mount of Beatitudes Chorazin*, with Ray Vandar Laan, Videocassette. Focus on the Family Films, Colorado,1996. 22 Min.
6. Isaiah 7:14.
7. Revelation 19:8.
8. Ephesians 5:27.
9. Matthew 25:1-13.
10. *Unger's Bible Dictionary*, by Merrill F. Unger, Chicago, 1974, p. 698.
11. Ibid.
12. Matthew 25:6, 7.
13. Unger, p. 698.
14. Ibid. p. 699.
15. Ibid.
16. Ephesians 5:26.
17. Luke 1:6.
18. Hebrews 11:17-19.
19. Genesis 22:1-19.

Chapter 2 Lord, Hear my Prayer

1. I Samuel 1:8.
2. I Samuel 1:6-8.
3. I Samuel 1:10-20.
4. Deuteronomy 6:5-7,9
5. *The Gospel of Luke* by William Barclay, Philadelphia, 1956, p. 4.
6. Genesis 25:21-27.
7. Malachi 3:6.
8. Genesis 18:1-15.

Chapter 3 Serving the Lord

1. Unger. p. 1079.
2. Ibid. p. 1080.
3. Ibid.
4. Malachi 4:5,6.
5. Barclay, p. 4.
6. *The Temple* by The Rev. Dr. Edersheim, New York, p. 87.
7. Barclay, p. 3.
8. Genesis 22:1-9.
9. Freeman, p. 359.
10. Edersheim, p. 89.
11. Joshua 14:8,9,14.
12. John 19:23b.
13. Edersheim, p. 97.
14. Proverbs 17:22.
15. Isaiah 30:15.

Chapter 4 A Heavenly Visitor

1. Barclay, p. 4.
2. Luke 1:11-13.
3. Ibid. v. 14.
4. Ibid. v. 15.
5. Ibid.
6. Ibid. v. 16.
7. Ibid. v. 17.

[8] Ibid. v. 18-20.
[9] Ibid. v. 21-23.
[10] Ibid. v. 24.
[11] Psalm 139:13b-16.
[12] Luke 1:25.

Chapter 5 A Visitor with a Heavenly Message

[1] Luke 1:41-45.
[2] Ibid. v. 46, 47.
[3] Romans 3:23.
[4] Luke 1:48-55.
[5] Ibid. v. 27.
[6] Ibid. v. 28.
[7] Ibid. v. 29-35.
[8] Isaiah 7:14.
[9] Ibid.
[10] Luke 1: 36-38.

Chapter 6 Lord, Help Us Understand How We Fit into Your Plan

[1] "Providence", poem by William Cowper, *Poems to be Read Aloud to Children and by Children,* edited by Ann McFerran, New York, 1965, p. 64.
[2] Romans 8:28.
[3] Ephesians 3:20.
[4] Luke 1:17.
[5] "Feasts of the O.T.: Their Historic, Christian and Prophetic Significance," syllabus by Dr. Grady McMurtry, Orlando, 1995, p. 2.
[6] Psalm 103:5.
[7] Romans 8:11.

Chapter 7 *He Shall be Called John*

[1] Ruth 4:17.
[2] Luke 1:60-62.
[3] Luke 1:63-67a.

Endnotes

4. Ibid. v. 67b-79.
5. *The Feasts of the Lord* by Kevin Howard and Marvin Rosenthal, Nashville, p. 59.
6. Matt 17:12.
7. Luke 1:17.

Chapter 8 What About Mary?

1. Unger, p. 698.
2. Matt. 1:19.
3. Ibid. v. 20-24.
4. Luke 1:28.
5. *The Language of the Culture, Sepphoris*, "That the World May Know" videocassette series, "Faith Lesson: 16" with Ray Vandar Laan, Focus on the Family, Colorado Springs, 1996, 20 min.

Chapter 9 *In the Fullness of Time*

1. Howard and Rosenthal, p. 137.
2. Ezekial 16:4.
3. "Lambs are born" article by James E. Smith II in the "Baptist Bulletin", Dec. 1979.
4. Dr. Grady McMurtry, phone interview, 27 May, 2001. Men in that culture did not help with births, plus there were plenty of women around so that Joseph more than likely enlisted one to help Mary.
5. *Silent Night*, song, words by Joseph Mohr, music by Franz Gruber, public domain.
6. John 3:16.
7. *Away in the Manger*, song by Martin Luther, public domain.

Chapter 10 Shepherds Seek the Lamb

1. Luke 2:8, 9.
2. Ibid. v. 10-12.
3. Ibid. v. 13,14. Please note: the scriptures do not say the angels <u>sang</u>, but they were <u>saying</u> praises.

[4] *Hark the Herald Angels Sing,* song by Charles Wesley, public domain.
[5] Luke 2:15.
[6] Ibid. v. 16.
[7] Ibid. v. 17-20.
[8] John 1:1-14a.
[9] *O Come, All Ye Faithful,* song by Tr. Fr. Oakeley, Wade's Cantus Diversi.
[10] *Hark the Herald Angels Sing,* song by Charles Wesley, 1739 and music by Felix Mendelssohn.

Chapter 11 Circumcision of the Baby

[1] Unger, p. 361, 362.

Chapter 12 Presentation in the Temple

[1] Luke 2:25-33.
[2] Ibid. v. 34-35.
[3] Ibid. v. 36-38.
[4] Matthew 1:25.

Chapter 13 A Star in the East

[1] Matthew 2:11.
[2] Luke 1:32-33.
[3] Luke 2:35.
[4] *We Three Kings of Orient Are,* by John Henry Hopkins, Jr., public domain.
[5] McMurty, p. 2.
[6] Matthew 2:2.
[7] Ibid. v.3.
[8] *The Narrated Bible, In Chronological Order, NIV,* Narration by F. LaGard Smith, Harvest House Publishers, Eugene, 1985, p. 1355.
[9] Matthew 2:4-6.
[10] Ibid. v. 7-9.
[11] Ibid. v. 10.
[12] *The First Noel,* Old English song, public domain.

[13] Matthew 2:12-14.
[14] Ibid. v. 16.
[15] McMurtry, p. 2.
[16] Genesis 22:13-14.
[17] Galatians 6:7.
[18] Matthew 2:19-21.

Chapter 14 Home at Last

[1] Matthew 2:22.
[2] Luke 2:39c.
[3] Galatians 1:19.

Appendices

A

Biblical Marriage Customs: A Picture of the Relationship of the Bride of Christ to Her Groom

God ordained marriage, establishing it *In the Beginning*:

In the beginning, Adam was given Eve for His wife
Genesis 2:21-24

Jesus continues His approval and blessing on marriage because *in the beginning* of His ministry He attended and performed His first miracle at the Wedding in Cana
John 2:1-11

1. Selection of the Bride by the Father of the Groom

The wife for Adam, the first husband, was selected by His Father, the Creator. Adam went to sleep; while the bride was prepared. His bride was born out of his side even as the bride of Christ was born by the water and the blood from His side, John 19:34. Often stated in marriage ceremonies is the saying, "the wife was not taken from Adam's head that she might rule over him, nor his feet that he might trample her, but from his side that he might have her by his side to love and cherish." The same is true of the church's relationship to her Husband in that she does not rule over Him, He rules over the church. The church was not taken from the Lord's feet that He would trample her but the blood and water from His side so that He loves and cherishes her.

God's design for marriage is one man married to one woman, which is shown in the first family. The fact that Eve is given the name of her husband is revealed in Genesis 5:2, *Male and female created he them; and blessed them, and called their name Adam, in the day when they were created.* A wife's identity, while separate and individual, is still inextricably entwined with her husbands'. Their union becomes a new creation with power in agreement unlike any other association. She wears his name. In earthly families, the wife takes on the name of her husband for the same reason and becomes one flesh with him even as the church becomes one with Jesus. The bride of Christ in being known as Christian has taken on His name. *For this cause shall a man leave his father and mother and shall be joined unto his wife and the two shall be one flesh. This is a great mystery: for I speak concerning Christ and the Church* Ephesians 5:31-32.

2. Betrothal/Espousal/Engagement

A. The Engagement was Arranged by the Father or a Legal Representative

In the story of the selection of a wife for Isaac by Abraham (Genesis 24) is also seen this beautiful parallel. Abraham (a type/picture of God the Father) sends forth His servant (a type of the Holy Spirit) to select a bride, Rebekah, (a type of the Church) for his son, Isaac (a type of the Son, Jesus).[1] Earlier in Genesis (chapter 22) the type is established for Abraham as God the Father when he sacrificed his only son Isaac, who represented Jesus.

While today the Holy Spirit is searching for and joining the bride to her groom, there are others representing the Father to the Bride. *John* [the Baptist and forerunner of Jesus] *said, He that*

Appendix A

hath the bride is the bridegroom: but the friend of the bridegroom, which stands and hears him, rejoices greatly because of the bridegroom's voice; this, my joy therefore is fulfilled. He must increase and I must decrease John 3:29. Paul is also seen working on behalf of the Father as a legal representative. He wrote, *For I am jealous over you with godly jealousy: for I have espoused you to one husband, that I may present you a chaste virgin to Christ* II Corinthians 11:2.

B. Involved in the Engagement was the Giving and Acceptance of Gifts, (Signifying Acceptance of the Proposal), and an Oath of Confirmation

In the selection of the bride, the servant brought gifts for the bride as a token of something greater to come. In Genesis 24 gifts were given to Rebekah as well as her family. This in a way represents later customs where the bride is sometimes considered purchased with gifts that were brought. The Church has entered into a relationship with her Groom and belongs to Him, And *you are not your own. For you are bought with a price: therefore glorify God in your body, and in your spirit, which are God's* I Corinthians 6:19b, 20.

Rebekah was consulted as to her willingness to become Isaac's bride. *And they called Rebekah, and said unto her, "Will you go with this man?" And she said, "I will go"* Genesis 24:58. Her acceptance of the proposal, the acceptance of the gifts along with an oath, confirmed the betrothal. The gift of the Holy Spirit, promised in Acts 2:38,39 and all He gives, are for this life as well as for something greater to come II Corinthians 5:5. Rebekah, the bride, (like Christians today) made the personal decision to accept the proposal to become Isaac's wife. Christians are those who have accepted the Lord's invitation, and enter into an oath/confession at salvation so that a formal relationship/betrothal is entered into with the Lord.

In other accounts of marriage in the Bible, espousal followed selection of the bride. It "was not altogether like our 'engagement,' but was a formal proceeding, undertaken by a friend or legal representative on the part of the bridegroom, and the parents on the part of the bride. It was confirmed by oaths, accompanied with presents to the bride...The act of betrothal was celebrated by a feast..."[2] Following the betrothal was the engagement period, which usually lasted a year.

C. Relationship during the Engagement

The man was known as the husband and the woman his wife during this time. *Now the birth of Jesus Christ was on this wise: When as his mother Mary was <u>espoused</u> to Joseph, before they came together, she was found with child of the Holy Spirit. Then Joseph <u>her husband</u>, being a just man and not willing to make her a public example, was minded <u>to put her away privately</u>. But while he thought on these things, behold, the angel of the lord appeared unto him in a dream, saying, Joseph thou son of David, fear not to take unto thee Mary <u>thy wife</u>: for that which is conceived in her is of the Holy Spirit* Matthew 1:18-20.

The union of the espoused husband and wife was so binding, it could only be broken by divorce or death, Matthew 1:18-20. There were no physical relationships during this time and no communication between them except through an intermediary, usually the friend of the bridegroom. The intercessor made known the husband and his plans to the wife. On the long journey back to Isaac's home, surely Rachel (a type of the bride of Christ) listened intently as the servant (a type of the Holy Spirit) told her about her groom. The Holy Spirit is revealing Jesus to His church /bride today John 14:26; 16:13,14. "The servant is the Holy Comforter, the Paraclete ('one called alongside of'), who accompanies the Church through the world's wilderness, teaching her the things of Christ and showing things to come, until finally He presents her to Christ at the end of the journey."[3]

The engaged bride in the Scriptures, while legally bound to her husband during this period, did not change her residence.

Appendix A

The church is still in the world although not of it, while she looks for the time she sees Him face to face and He takes her out. Jesus prayed, *And now I am no more in the world, but <u>these are in the world</u>, and I come to thee…*John 17:11a. *They are not of the world, even as I am not of the world* John 17:16. *For now we see through a glass darkly, but then <u>face to face</u>* I Corinthians 13:12.

D. The Husband's Role and Wife's Role During Engagement Period

The husband prepares a place to take his bride; the place usually being a room adjacent to his father's house. The father could oversee the work, know when it was finished and send his son for the bride.[4] Jesus said, *In my Father's house are many mansions* [some versions read "rooms"]: *if it were not so, I would have told you. <u>I go to prepare a place for you</u>. And if I go and prepare a place for you, I will come again, and receive you unto myself; that <u>where I am, there you may be also</u>* John 14:2,3.

The wife prepares herself and her wedding garment. *Let us be glad and rejoice, and give honour to him: for the marriage of the Lamb is come, and <u>his wife has made herself ready</u>. And to her was granted that <u>she should be arrayed in fine linen, clean and white</u>: for the fine linen is the righteousness of saints* Revelation 19:7,8. *And I John saw the holy city, new Jerusalem, coming down from God out of heaven, <u>prepared as a bride adorned for her husband</u>* Revelation 21:2.

The wife does not know <u>when</u> but she does knows he <u>will</u> come to take her away. The story of the wise and foolish virgins in Matthew 25:1-13 pictures this: *While the bridegroom tarried, they all slumbered and slept. And at midnight there was a cry made, Behold, the bridegroom comes; go ye out to meet him* Matthew 25:5,6. *<u>Watch therefore, for you know neither the day nor the hour wherein the Son of man comes</u>* Matthew 25:13.

3. The Wedding Celebration

A. Wedding Garments

The kingdom of heaven is like unto a certain king, which made a marriage for his son...he sent forth his servants to call them that were bidden to the wedding..." Behold, I have prepared my dinner...all things are ready, come unto the marriage"...And when the king came in to see the guests, he saw <u>there a man, which had not a wedding garment</u>..., and cast him to outer darkness Matthew 22:1-14.

B. Times of the Celebration

The bridegroom often came at night and unexpectedly...illustrated by the parable of the virgins. *While the bridegroom tarried, they all slumbered and slept. And <u>at midnight there was a cry made, Behold, the bridegroom cometh</u>; go ye out to meet him..." Watch therefore, for ye know neither the day nor the hour wherein the Son of man cometh* Matthew 25:5,6,13.

The Wedding Feast usually lasted a week. Genesis 29 illustrates this, *And Jacob said unto Laban, "Give me my wife, for my days are fulfilled, that I may go in unto her." And Laban gathered together all the men of the place and made a feast...*v. 21,22. *And it came to pass in the evening that he took Leah his daughter, and brought her to him; and he went in unto her* v. 23. The festivities were to last a week longer in that Laban told Jacob in v. 27 <u>*to fulfil her week*</u>.

C. Festivities

"The essence of the [wedding] ceremony consisted in the removal of the bride from her father's house to that of the bridegroom or his father. There seems, indeed, to be a literal truth in the Hebrew expression 'to take' a wife (Numbers 12:1; I Chronicles 2:21, marg.), for the ceremony appears to have mainly consisted in the taking.

Appendix A

"After putting on a festive dress, placing a handsome turban on his head (Isaiah 61:10, A.V. 'ornaments') and a nuptial crown (Cant. 3:11), the bridegroom sets forth from his house, attended by his groomsmen (A.V. 'companions,' Judge.14:11; 'children of the bride-chamber,' Matthew 9:15), preceded by a band of musicians or singers (Genesis 31:27; Jeremiah 7:34; 16:9; I MACC. 9:39), and accompanied by persons bearing flambeaus (II Esdr. 10:2; Matthew 25:7; comp. Jeremiah 25:10; Revelation 18:23, 'the light of a candle'). Having reached the house of the bride, who with her maidens anxiously expected his arrival (Matthew 25:6), he conducted the whole party back to his own or his father's house, with every demonstration of gladness (Psalm 45:15). On their way back they were joined by a party of maidens, friends of the bride and bridegroom, who were in waiting to catch the procession as it passed (Matthew 25:6). The inhabitants of the place pressed out into the streets to watch the procession. (Cant. 3:11). At the house a feast was prepared, to which all the friends and neighbors were invited (Genesis 29:22; Matthew 22:1-10; Luke 14:8; John 2:2), and the festivities were protracted for seven, or even 14, days (Judges 14:12; Tob. 8:19). The guests were provided by the host with fitting robes (Matt. 22:11), and the feast was enlivened with riddles (Judges 14:12) and other amusements. The bridegroom now entered into direct communication with the bride, and the joy of the friend was 'fulfilled' at hearing the voice of the bridegroom (John 3:29) conversing with her, which he regarded as a satisfactory testimony of the success of his share in the work. The last act in the ceremonial was the conducting of the bride to the bridal chamber, (Heb. *heder*, Judges 15:1; Joel 2:16), where a canopy, named *huppah*, was prepared (Psalm 19:5; Joel 2:16)."[5]

For the Lord himself shall descend from heaven with a shout, with the voice of the archangel, and with the trump of God and the dead in Christ shall rise first: Then we which are alive and remain shall be caught up together with them in the clouds, to meet the Lord in the air: and so shall we ever be with the Lord I Thessalonians 4:16-17.

D. The Marriage Supper

And he saith unto me, "Write, Blessed are they which are called unto <u>the marriage supper of the Lamb</u>" Revelation 19:9.

4. Conclusion: ONE Family for Eternity

Husband and wife relationships here on earth give us a picture of the marriage to come between Christ and His bride but the natural relationships between husband and wife here on earth do not extend into heaven. Termination of relationship is at death. *The wife is bound by the law as long as her husband liveth; but if her husband be dead, she is at liberty to be married to whom she will...* I Corinthians 7:39.

For in the resurrection <u>they neither marry, nor are given in marriage</u>, but are as the angels of God in heaven Matthew 22:30. This scripture fully points out that there are not families (plural) for eternity because there is only ONE family in heaven and that is the family of God.

The Church as the bride of Christ will rule and reign with Him. The church is not a group of people now or for eternity but a family; which is rightfully defined as "those related by the marriage of one man to one woman, by blood or adoption". On all three counts the church fits the definition of family. The church is an eternally related family by the marriage of the one body, I Corinthians 12:12,13, the bride of Christ (the Church) to her Groom. The family is related by blood (the blood of Christ) and adoption. *For you have received the Spirit of <u>adoption</u>.* Romans 8:15.

God's plan for marriage is a covenant, not a contract, Malachi 2:14,15. Contracts are based on distrust and can be broken. Covenants are based on trust and are to be permanent. So the Church rejoices now that her eternal covenant marriage to her Lord, Jesus Christ, has begun on earth with the betrothal/espousal. She rejoices knowing that one day she will see Him face to face when

Appendix A

he comes to take her out of this world for the marriage supper *And so they shall ever be with the Lord* I Thessalonians 4:17! *And the Spirit and <u>the bride</u> say, Come* Revelation 22:17.

He which testifieth these things saith, "Surely I come quickly." Amen. Even so, come, Lord Jesus Revelation 22:20. Maranatha!

Endnotes

1. *The Genesis Record,* by Dr. Henry Morris, p. 391.
2. *Unger's Bible Dictionary,* by Merrill Unger, p. 698.
3. Morris, p. 405.
4. *That the Word May Know"* series, *Faith Lession 14: No Greater Love/Mount of Beatitudes Chorazin,* with Ray Vandar Lann, Videoccassette, Focus on the Family Films, Colorado Springs, 1996. 22 min.
5. Unger, p. 698.

B
Praying for Children/Grandchildren: How to Pray and to Develop a Prayer Notebook for Children

And there was one Anna, the prophetess, the daughter of Phanuel, of the tribe of Aser: she was a great age, and had lived with an husband seven years from her virginity: And she was a widow of about fourscore and four years which departed not from the temple, but served God with fastings and prayers night and day. And she coming in that instant gave thanks likewise unto the Lord, and spake of him [the baby Jesus] *to all them that looked for redemption in Jerusalem.*

And when they [Mary and Joseph] *had performed things according to the law of the Lord, they returned into Galilee, to their own city Nazareth, and the child* [Jesus] *grew, and waxed strong in spirit, filled with wisdom; and the grace of God was upon him.* Luke 2:36-40

It has been suggested that the prayers of Anna the prophetess protected the Baby Jesus through those first few years of His life when Herod ordered all boy babies two years old and below killed. While the scriptures do not exactly state Anna as being His intercessor, many times the Lord raises up an intercessor(s) to pray before threatening events. These intercessors are sometimes allowed to be a part of the answer and/or to see the object of their prayers, which could very well be the case of Anna and Baby Jesus.

Appendix B

Today there is a great destruction aimed at children. This should place an urgency of continuing intercession on parents and grandparents! Just as adults are encouraged knowing someone is praying for them; likewise, children need encouragement by knowing that someone is praying for them. They also need to know what has been prayed and what is being prayed for them.

In 1986, when our daughter, Julie, and her husband announced to my husband and me that they were expecting a baby (our first grandchild) the Lord led me to begin a grandmother's prayer notebook. I began to look for scriptures to pray for the child and wrote them out...not only to build a wall of prayer around the child while yet in the womb, but also to build a wall for the future. In time I wanted my grandchild not only to know I had been praying for him before he was born, but also to know *what* had been prayed so that his faith would be strong.

This prayer project brought a greater depth in prayer and new understanding of scriptures for me as the Holy Spirit gave me insight and revelation. As I wrote out the scriptures, then prayed them repeatedly, I suddenly realized that I was memorizing scriptures and receiving insight without making that an objective! I had set out to bless another and was blessed myself.

As time passed I developed a very close relationship with this unborn child. I came to believe that he would be strong and mighty in the Lord because of the scriptures I had been led to pray. I also saw in a new way the Spirit's involvement with the unborn (Psalm 139:13-16), the newly born (Isaiah 49:1b) and with little children. Also, a revelation was that these little ones, fresh from God, have not only bodies that need nourishing, but spirits, too!

After that glorious occasion of the baby's birth and while our daughter was still in the hospital, I encouraged her to read scriptures to her baby, Brett, every day because *newborn babes desire the sincere milk of the Word. Faith cometh by hearing and hearing by the word of God,* and Brett is going to be "a man of faith". (The Bible reading would bless her, too.)

A few weeks later, on the way to the baby's dedication, I asked the Lord for confirmation of the prayer notebook and all I had been praying. During the dedication prayer for the baby, one of the leaders of the church began to weep as he prayed and said that he believed Brett was going to be "a man of faith!" That church leader knew nothing of my prayer notebook or my conversation with Julie.

Hopefully, at this point, the need for and the blessings that come from spending time in searching the scriptures, recording and praying them in behalf of children/grandchildren are apparent. Here are a few suggestions to help get started:

- Use a looseleaf notebook with dividers and a section for each child. (This is obviously a way to pray for children already born and those not yet conceived.) Set aside a few minutes daily or a larger portion of time weekly to research and pray. This prayer project will be developed over time and can be a life time project, so take your time and allow the Lord to speak to you as you pray, meditate and develop this notebook. This may involve replacing TV time with prayer time for the family. You will be eternally grateful you did.
- Write the scriptures exactly as found in the Bible. Remember, you will be memorizing without trying, so you will want to be accurate. Then, write the scripture as a prayer below it and make a note of the date. For example:

    "Lord, I'm asking You, in Jesus' name, to help this child grow, wax strong in spirit, be filled with wisdom, having Your grace upon him. Thank You for answering this prayer." 4/2/92
- As your notebook develops, you probably will not be praying every scripture every prayer time, but you will have some direction and depth of content when you do pray. However, you may want to establish a family tradition of praying all or some of these scriptures on his/her birthday each year.

Appendix B

What a heritage for your children as one day you hand them their portion of the notebook and say, "These are the scriptures I have been praying for you for years!" Wouldn't you be encouraged today to have such a notebook of prayers from your mother/grandmother?!

> *This shall be recorded for the generation to come; and the people which shall be created shall praise the Lord.* Psalm 102:18
>
> Isaiah 40:11c A scripture for the expectant mom. "Lord, gently lead this mom as she is 'with young.'"
>
> Isaiah 49:25b *for I will contend with him that contends with you, and I will save your children.*
>
> Isaiah 49:1b *The Lord has called me from the womb, from the body of my mother He has made mention of my name.* "Lord, You name this baby."

As I was praying this for our oldest daughter, Valerie, I dated the entry in my notebook. Later, I discovered that she and her husband were naming the baby during that time! The baby's name is Andrew Rose. Andrew in the Gospels was the one who brought people to Jesus. I'm trusting the Lord to use this grandchild as an evangelist, too, because the Good News of Jesus' glorious resurrection is proclaimed in this grandson's name: Andy Rose…"And He rose." Praise the Lord!

> Judges 13:8,9 teach *us what we are to do unto the child that shall be born.* "Lord, teach this child's parents how to rear him according to Your ways and Your plan for his life."
> Mark 12:29-32 "May this child love You with all his heart, soul, mind, strength and his neighbor as himself."

I Thessalonians 5:23 "Lord, help this child's spirit and soul and body to be found sound and blameless at Your coming."

Proverbs 2:1-7 "May this child seek You, as these scriptures show how, so the child may have the fear of the Lord which is the beginning of wisdom and knowledge. May his education begin with the fear of the Lord."

Job 28:29 "May this child never be entertained by evil media so that he will have understanding."

Matthew 24:4-5 "Keep him from deception."

Exodus 35:31 *And he has filled him with the Spirit of God, in wisdom, in understanding, and in knowledge and in all manner of workmanship.*

Salvation John 1:12,13; John 3:16; Romans 10:8,9; Acts 2:38

Prayers of the Apostle Paul These are great! Write them out and pray them regularly! Ephesians 1:16-23; 3:14-21; Colossians 1:9-14.

Daily Walk Mark 12:30-31; Ecclesiastes 12:13; I Corinthians 10:13; Mark 8:34; Romans 8 Lots of good verses here for a Spirit-led life. Choose the verses that speak to you.

Faith Hebrews 11:1, 6; II Peter 1:5-8.

Love I Corinthians 13:1-7

Purity Psalm 119:9-11

Appendix B

<u>Meditation on the Word</u> Psalm 1; Joshua 1:8

<u>Good character qualities</u> Look for scriptures that summarize godly lives, such as Joseph (Genesis 39:2,4,9c), Noah (Genesis 6:22, 7:5-16), Daniel (Daniel 5:14), and pray for those qualities to be developed in this child's life.

Continue searching for scriptures for this child's church, home, education, future spouse (should it be the Lord's will for this child to marry), health, finances, vocation, the civil government under which he will live, protection from sexual sins and assaults.

As you see, this is only a beginning. You will be led to many other scriptures. While there are some scriptures that are foundational to all children, you may find you have direction to pray specific scriptures for different children as the Lord begins to direct you into praying for each child's individuality.

The hour is late and the need for intercessors is urgent! You and your children and/or grandchildren will be eternally grateful for your time in prayer for them.

This method of writing out scriptures and praying them is not limited to praying just for your children. Consider doing the same for other members of the family and children not related to you who need an intercessor. The world needs more "Bereans" who will search the Word daily not only for themselves, but on behalf of their families, and others, too! Acts 11:10-12.

So shall my word be that goes forth out of my mouth: it shall not return unto me void, but it shall accomplish that which I please... Isaiah 55:11

I thank God...that without ceasing I have remembrance of you in my prayers night and day. When I call to remembrance the unfeigned faith that is in you, which dwelt first in your grandmother, Lois, and your mother, Eunice... II Timothy 1:3, 5

C

Study Suggestions for the Scriptures on the Births of John the Baptist and Jesus

Start a notebook for this study. Not only will there be topics here to study but through the years; esp., at the Christmas season, there will be insights and stories too good to forget. These should be added to the notebook.

Always start with prayer asking for *a spirit of wisdom and revelation* Ephesians 1:17.

For a thorough study of these births, copy the following Scriptures from a good study version of the Bible (not a paraphrase). This has been done in the KJV in appendix D. For a worksheet format it should be doubled spaced with wide margins for notes and lines before each major section for writing a title. There should be enough space after each section for writing out names of characters, places and times. The following references are given in the chronological order:

Luke 1:5-25	Matthew 1:25
Luke 1:26-38	Luke 2:8-20
Luke 1:39-45	Luke 2:21
Luke 1:46-56	Luke 2:22-38
Luke 1:57-80	Matthew 2:1-11
Matthew 1:18-24	Matthew 2:12-18, 21-23
Luke 2:1-7	Luke 2:39

(Get a copy of Kay Arthur's book, <u>How to Study Your Bible</u>, Harvest House Publishers, 1994, at a Christian bookstore and do observation worksheets on these verses by identifying the Who, What, Where, When, etc., making titles and marking the key words. Also do topic and character studies suggested in her book. You will be blessed.)

The following topics are suggested studies. Bible classes or homeschoolers might want each student to take just one topic and then report back to the class/family. Individuals who study all the topics will be blessed with a thorough understanding of these two births. During their studies, each student of the Word will probably see other topics to study.

1. Father/Son/ Holy Spirit

What do these scriptures teach concerning each member of the Godhead?
Write out the various names given to Jesus, along with who gave it and the verse.
What can be learned about God's character?
Knowing His character, how does this relate to a person's life today?

2. Angels

What can be learned about angels from these scriptures; their work, where they have been seen, what was said, their relationship to God and to man?

3. Prophecies

Identify Old Testament prophecies and their fulfillment in the births of John the Baptist and Jesus. (Many are listed as cross references in most Bibles.)

Appendix C

Study the prophecies given by Zacharias and Mary. Were any fulfilled?
What can be learned about God's character in the fulfillment of these prophecies?

4. Jesus' Genealogy

Compare the genealogy of Jesus in Matthew 1:2-17 to the one in Luke 3:23-38.
How are they similar?
How are they different?

5. Maps and Historical Background

On a map of Israel during the time of Christ, identify places of the events.
The Word says, *But when the fulness of the time was come, God sent forth his son, made of a woman...*Galatians 4:4 Consult reference books to find out what events occurred during the 400 years between the Old and New Testaments that contributed to the fulness of time when Christ came (the prepared/right time for Christ to be born).

6. Characters (Do not include civil rulers. These will be listed under the next heading.)

Identify all persons mentioned in these verses and what can be learned about them.
Pay special attention to their character, words and theology; i.e., their belief in God as expressed by themselves or what others say about them. Make notes.

7. Civil Rulers

Identify their position in government ... how they ruled, etc.

What can be learned about life in a pagan form of civil government under which these people lived and its effect on their lives? Note the results of living under a government where rulers had absolute power, made their own laws with no accountability to the people and where people feared their government.

Contrast that to life under the Christian form of civil government America had at the founding of the nation where the government had limited power, was accountable to the people who were under God, laws were enacted by representatives of the people and governing principles were based on the Word of God.

8. Customs

What customs of the day are identified in these scriptures that are necessary to understanding the story?

9. Mosaic Law

Obtain a diagram of the temple, find the locations of events mentioned in these verses.

What references to keeping the Mosaic Law are mentioned in these verses?

Find these verses in Matthew and Luke and look up any cross-references to the Mosaic law, and read them.

Identify the Feasts mentioned here and look in reference books for more information.

10. Key Words/Phrases

Identify, mark and make lists of key words/phrases (major words or phrases repeated often) and how they are used.

11. Definitions

Make a list of words, along with their definitions, which gives a better understanding of these verses. Use a concordance for the original Greek words and/or use <u>Webster's 1828 Dictionary.</u>

12. Prayer, Praises and Insights

How did this study help in knowing Jesus, Who He is, and how to refute cults that say He is not God or that His father was not Deity.

Write out praises and prayers in these verses for personal worship today.

Write out insights that came concerning your personal walk with the Lord.

D

Bible Verses from Luke and Matthew on The Births of John the Baptist and Jesus

Readers are encouraged to read the following verses that tell of the births of John the Baptist and Jesus and have been placed in the generally accepted chronological order. Except for titles, which have been added at the beginning of each section, this part contains only Bible verses. It is important that everyone leave this book with a clear understanding of the difference in what the Bible actually says and what was personal commentary by the author.

The following verses come from the King James Version of the Bible, although certain outdated terms; such as, ye, thee, thou, etc. have been updated. The term "Holy Ghost" has been changed to "Holy Spirit".

Luke 1:5-25 Angelic Announcement to Zacharias

There was in the days of Herod, the king of Judea, a certain priest named Zacharias, of the course of Abia: and his wife was of the daughters of Aaron, and her name was Elisabeth. And they were both righteous before God, walking in all the commandments and ordinances of the Lord blameless. And they had no child, because that Elisabeth was barren, and they both were now well stricken in years.

And it came to pass, that while he executed the priest's office before God in the order of his course, according to the custom of the priest's office, his lot was to burn incense when he went into the temple of the Lord. And the whole multitude of the people were praying without at the time of incense.

And there appeared unto him an angel of the Lord standing on the right side of the altar of incense. And when Zacharias saw him, he was troubled, and fear fell upon him. But the angel said unto him, fear not, Zacharias: for your prayer is heard; and your wife Elisabeth shall bear you a son, and you shall call his name John. And you shall have joy and gladness; and many shall rejoice at his birth. For he shall be great in the sight of the Lord, and shall drink neither wine nor strong drink; and he shall be filled with the Holy Spirit, even from his mother's womb. And many of the children of Israel shall he turn to the Lord their God. And he shall go before him in the spirit and power of Elijah, to turn the hearts of the fathers to the children, and the disobedient to the wisdom of the just; to make ready a people prepared for the Lord.

And Zacharias said unto the angel, Whereby shall I know this? for I am an old man, and my wife well stricken in years. And the angel answering said unto him, I am Gabriel, that stand in the presence of God; and am sent to speak to you, and to show you these glad tidings. And, behold, you shall be dumb and not able to speak, until the day that these things shall be performed, because you believed not my words, which shall be fulfilled in their season. And the people waited for Zacharias, and marveled that he tarried so long in the temple. And when he came out, he could not speak to them: And they perceived that he had seen a vision in the temple: for he beckoned unto them, and remained speechless.

And it came to pass, that as soon as the days of his ministration were accomplished, he departed to his own house. And after those days his wife Elisabeth conceived, and hid herself five months, saying, Thus has the Lord dealt with me in the days wherein he looked on me, to take away my reproach among men.

Luke 1:26-38 Gabriel's Announcement to Mary

And in the sixth month the angel Gabriel was sent from God unto a city of Galilee, named Nazareth, To a virgin espoused to a man whose name was Joseph, of the house of David; and the virgin's name was Mary. And the angel came unto her, and said, Hail, you are highly favored, the Lord is with you: blessed are you among women. And when she saw him, she was troubled at his saying, and cast in her mind what manner of salutation this should be.

Appendix D

And the angel said to her, Fear not, Mary: for you have found favor with God. And, behold, you shall conceive in you womb, and bring forth a son, and shall call his name JESUS. He shall be great, and shall be called the Son of the Highest: and the Lord God shall give to him the throne of his father David: And he shall reign over the house of Jacob forever; and of his kingdom there shall be no end.

Then said Mary to the angel, How shall this be, seeing I know not a man? And the angel answered and said to her, The Holy Spirit shall come upon you, and the power of the Highest shall overshadow you: therefore also that holy thing which shall be born of you shall be called the Son of God. And behold, your cousin, Elisabeth, she has also conceived a son in her old age: and this is the sixth month with her, who was called barren, For with God nothing shall be impossible.

And Mary said, Behold the handmaid of the Lord; Be it unto me according to your word. And the angel departed from her.

Luke 1:39-45 Mary's Visit with Elisabeth

And Mary arose in those days, and went into the hill country with haste into a city of Juda; And entered into the house of Zacharias, and saluted Elisabeth. And it came to pass, that, when Elisabeth heard the salutation of Mary, the babe leaped in her womb; and Elisabeth was filled with the Holy Spirit: And she spoke out with a loud voice, and said, Blessed are you among women, and blessed is the fruit of your womb. And what is this to me, that the mother of my Lord should come to me? For, lo, as soon as the voice of your salutation sounded in mine ears, the babe leaped in my womb for joy. And blessed is she that believed: for there shall be a performance of those things which were told her from the Lord.

Luke 1:46-56 Mary's Psalm of Praise

And Mary said, My soul does magnify the Lord, And my spirit has rejoiced in God my Saviour. For he has regarded the low estate of his handmaiden: for, behold, from henceforth all generations shall call me blessed. For he that is mighty has done to me great things; and holy is his name. And his mercy is on them that fear him from generation to generation. He has shown strength with his arms; he has scattered the proud in the imagination of their hearts. He has put down the mighty from their seats, and exalted them of low degree. He has filled the hungry with good things; and the rich he has sent empty away. He has given help to his servant Israel, in remembrance of his mercy; As he spoke to our fathers, to Abraham, and to his seed forever.

And Mary abode with her about three months, and returned to her own house.

APPENDIX D

Luke 1:57-80 John the Baptist's Birth

Now Elisabeth's full time came that she should be delivered; and she brought forth a son. And her neighbours and her cousins heard how the Lord had shown great mercy upon her; and they rejoiced with her. And it came to pass, that on the eighth day they came to circumcise the child; and they called him Zacharias, after the name of his father.

And his mother answered and said, Not so; but he shall be called John. And they said to her, There is none of your kindred that is called by this name. And they made signs to his father, how he would have him called. And he asked for a writing tablet, and wrote, saying, His name is John. And they marvelled all. And his mouth was opened immediately, and his tongue loosed, and he spoke, and praised God.

And fear came on all that dwelt round about them: and all these sayings were noised abroad throughout all the hill country of Judea. And all they that heard them laid them up in their hearts, saying, What manner of child shall this be! And the hand of the Lord was with him.

And his father Zacharias was filled with the Holy Spirit, and prophesied, saying, Blessed be the Lord God of Israel; for he has visited and redeemed his people, And has raised up an horn of salvation for us in the house of his servant David; As he spoke by the mouth of his holy prophets, which have been since the world began: That we should be saved from our enemies, and from the hand of all that hate us; To perform the mercy promised to our fathers, and to remember his holy covenant; The oath which he swear to our father Abraham, That he would grant unto us, that we being delivered out of the hand of our enemies might serve him without fear, In holiness and righteousness before him, all the days of our life. You, child, shall be called the prophet of the Highest: for you shall go before the face of the Lord to prepare his ways; To give knowledge of salvation unto his people by the remission of their sins, Through the tender mercy of our God; whereby the dayspring from on high has visited us, To give light to them that sit in darkness and in the shadow of death, to guide our feet into the way of peace.

And the child grew and waxed strong in spirit, and was in the deserts till the day of his showing unto Israel.

Matthew 1:18-24 The Angel's Announcement to Joseph

Now the birth of Jesus Christ was on this wise: When as his mother Mary was espoused to Joseph, before they came together, she was found with child of the Holy Spirit. Then Joseph her husband, being a just man, and not willing to make her a public example, was minded to put her away privately.

But while he thought on these things, behold, the angel of the Lord appeared unto him in a dream, saying,

APPENDIX D

Joseph, thou son of David, fear not to take unto yourself Mary your wife: for that which is conceived in her is of the Holy Spirit. And she shall bring forth a son, and you shall call his name JESUS: for he shall save his people from their sins.

Now all this was done, that it might be fulfilled which was spoken of the Lord by the prophet, saying, Behold, a virgin shall be with child, and shall bring forth a son, and they shall call his name Emmanuel, which being interpreted is, God with us. Then Joseph being raised from sleep did as the angel of the Lord had bidden him, and took unto him his wife: And knew her not till she had brought forth her first born son: and he called his name JESUS.

Luke 2:1-7 Birth of Jesus

And it came to pass in those days, that there went out a decree from Caesar Augustus, that all the world should be taxed. (And this taxing was first made when Cyrenius was governor of Syria.) And all went to be taxed, everyone into his own city. And Joseph also went up from Galilee, out of the city of Nazareth, into Judea, unto the city of David, which is called Bethlehem; (because he was of the house and lineage of David:) To be taxed with Mary his espoused wife, being great with child.

And so it was, that, while they were there, the days were accomplished that she should be delivered. And she brought forth her first born son, and wrapped him in swaddling clothes, and laid him in a manger; because there was no room for them in the inn.

Luke 2:8-20 Shepherds Come to Worship the Baby

And there were in the same country shepherds abiding in the field, keeping watch over their flock by night. And, lo, the angel of the Lord came upon them, and the glory of the Lord shown round about them: and they were sore afraid.

And the angel said unto them, Fear not: for, behold, I bring you good tidings of great joy, which shall be to all people. For unto you is born this day in the city of David a Savior, which is Christ the Lord. And this shall be a sign unto you; You shall find the babe wrapped in swaddling clothes, lying in a manger. And suddenly there was with the angel a multitude of the heavenly host praising God, and saying, Glory to God in the highest, and on earth peace, goodwill toward men.

And it came to pass, as the angels were gone away from them into heaven, the shepherds said one to another, Let us now go even unto Bethlehem, and see this thing which is come to pass, which the Lord has made known unto us. And they came with haste, and found Mary, and Joseph, and the babe lying in the manger. And when they had seen it, they made known abroad the saying which was told them concerning this child. And all they that heard it wondered at those things which were told them by the shepherds.

But Mary kept all these things and pondered them in her heart. And the shepherds returned, glorifying and praising God for all the things that they had heard and seen, as it was told unto them.

Luke 2:21 The Circumcision and Naming of Jesus

And when eight days were accomplished for the circumcising of the child, his name was called JESUS, which was so named of the angel before he was conceived in the womb.

Luke 2:22-38 Presentation in the Temple

And when the days of her purification according to the law of Moses were accomplished, they brought him to Jerusalem, to present him to the Lord; (As it is written in the law of the Lord, Every male that opens the womb shall be called holy to the Lord;) And to offer a sacrifice according to that which is said in the law of the Lord, A pair of turtledoves, or two young pigeons.

And, behold, there was a man in Jerusalem, whose name was Simeon; and the same man was just and devout, waiting for the consolation of Israel: and the Holy Spirit was upon him. And it was revealed unto him by the Holy Spirit, that he should not see death, before he had seen the Lord's Christ.

And he came by the Spirit into the temple: and when the parents brought in the child Jesus, to do for him after the custom of the law, Then took he him up in his arms, and blessed God, and said, Lord, now let your servant depart in peace, according to your word: For mine eyes have seen your salvation, which your have prepared before the face of all people; A light to lighten the Gentiles, and the glory of your people Israel. And Joseph and his mother marvelled at those things which were spoken of him.

And Simeon blessed them, and said unto Mary his mother, Behold, this child is set for the fall and rising again of many in Israel; and for a sign which shall be spoken against; (Yea, a sword shall pierce through your own soul also,) that the thoughts of many hearts may be revealed.

And there was one Anna, a prophetess, the daughter of Phanuel, of the tribe of Aser: she was of a great age, and had lived with an husband seven years from her virginity; And she was a widow of about fourscore and four years, which departed not from the temple, but served God with fastings and prayers night and day. And she coming in that instant gave thanks likewise unto the Lord, and spoke of him to all them that looked for redemption in Jerusalem.

Matthew 2:1-12 The Visit of the Wise Men

Now when Jesus was born in Bethlehem of Judea in the days of Herod the king, behold, there came wise men from the east to Jerusalem, Saying, Where is he that is born King of the Jews? For we have seen his star in the east, and are come to worship him.

When Herod the king had heard these things, he was troubled, and all Jerusalem with him. And when he had gathered all the chief priests and scribes of the people together, he demanded of them where Christ should be born. And they said unto him, In Bethlehem of Judea: for thus it is written by the prophet, And thou Bethlehem, in the land of Juda, art not the least among the princes of Juda: for out of thee shall come a Governor, that shall rule my people Israel.

Then Herod, when he had privately called the wise men, enquired of them diligently what time the star appeared. And he sent them to Bethlehem, and said, Go and search diligently for the young child; and when you have found him, bring me word again, that I may come and worship him also.

When they had heard the king, they departed; and, lo, the star, which they saw in the east, went before them, till it came and stood over where the young child was. And when they saw the star, they rejoiced with exceeding great joy.

And when they were come into the house, they saw the young child with Mary his mother, and fell down, and worshiped him: and when they had opened their treasures, they presented unto him gifts; gold, frankincense, and myrrh.

And being warned of God in a dream, that they should not return to Herod, they departed into their own country in another way.

Matthew 2:13-20   Flight into Egypt and Death of Herod

And when they were departed, behold, the angel of the Lord appeared to Joseph in a dream, saying, Arise, and take the young child and his mother, and flee into Egypt, and be there until I bring you word: for Herod will seek the young child to destroy him.

When he arose, he took the young child and his mother by night, and departed into Egypt: And was there until the death of Herod: that it might be fulfilled which was spoken of the Lord by the prophet, saying, Out of Egypt have I called my son.

Then Herod, when he saw that he was mocked of the wise men, was exceeding wroth, and sent forth, and slew all the children that were in Bethlehem, and in all the coasts thereof, from two years old and under, according to time which he had diligently enquired of the wise men.

Then was fulfilled that which was spoken by Jeremy the prophet, saying, In Rama was there a voice heard, lamentation, and weeping, and great mourning, Rachel weeping for her children, and would not be comforted, because they are not.

But when Herod was dead, behold, an angel of the Lord appeared in a dream to Joseph in Egypt, Saying, Arise, and take the young child and his mother, and go into the land of Israel: for they are dead which sought the young child's life.

Matthew 2:21-23 From Egypt to Nazareth

And he arose, and took the young child and his mother, and came into the land of Israel. But when he heard that Archelaus did reign in Judaea in the room of his father Herod, he was afraid to go there: notwithstanding, being warned of God in a dream, he turned aside into the parts of Galilee:

And he came and dwelt in a city called Nazareth: that it might be fulfilled which was spoken by the prophets, He shall be called a Nazarene.

Luke 2:40 Jesus' Childhood

And the child grew, and waxed strong in spirit, filled with wisdom and the grace of God was upon him.

Bibliography

The Bible, King James Version. Antiquated terms with updated phrases by Betty B. Howard.

Arthur, Kay. *How to Study Your Bible, The Lasting Rewards of the Inductive Approach*. Eugene: Harvest House, 1994.

Barclay, William. *The Gospel of Luke*. Philadelphia: The Westminster Press, 1956.

Cowper, William. poem, "Providence," McFerran, Ann, ed., *Poems to be Read Aloud to Children and by Children,* A Rutledge Book. New York: Thomas Nelson & Sons, 1965.

Edersheim, The Rev. Dr. *The Temple*. New York: Hodder & Stoughton.

Freeman, James M. *Manners and Customs of the Bible*, Plainfield, NJ: Logos International, 1972.

Howard, Kevin & Rosenthal, Marvin. *The Feasts of the Lord, God's Prophetic Calendar from Calvary to the Kingdom*. Nashville: Thomas Nelson, Inc., 1997.

McMurtry, Dr. Grady, syllabus, "Feasts of the O.T.: Their Historic Christian and Prophetic Significance", Orlando, FL, 1995.

Bibliography

Smith, F. LaGard. *The Narrated Bible.* Eugene: Harvest House, 1984.

Smith, James E., II. paper, "Where the Lambs are Born", "The Baptist Bulletin", December, 1979.

Unger, Merrill F. *Unger's Bible Dictionary.* Chicago: Moody Press, 1974.

Vandar Laan, Ray, "That the World May Know", series, "Faith Lesson 14: No Greater Love, Mount of Beatitudes/Chorazin", Videocassette, Focus on the Family Films, Colorado Springs, CO, 1996. 22 min.

Vander Laan, Ray, "That the World May Know" series, "Faith Lesson 16: The Language Of the Culture/ Sepphoris", Videocassette, Focus on the Family Films, Colorado Springs, CO, 1996. 20 min.